# TEACHER'S PET PUBLICATIONS

PUZZLE PACK
for
The Pearl

based on the book by
John Steinbeck

Written by
William T. Collins

© 2005 Teacher's Pet Publications
All Rights Reserved

The materials in this packet are copyrighted
by Teacher's Pet Publications, Inc.

These pages may be duplicated by the purchaser
for use in the purchaser's own classroom.

Copying any of these materials and distributing them
for any other purpose is a violation of the copyright laws.

© 2005 Teacher's Pet Publications, Inc.
www.tpet.com

INTRODUCTION
If you already own the LitPlan for this title, this Puzzle Pack will refresh your Unit Resource Materials and Vocabulary Resource Materials sections plus give you additional materials you can substitute into the tests. If you do not already have a complete LitPlan, these pages will give you some supplemental materials to use with your own plan. There are two main groups of materials: one set for unit words (such as characters' names, symbols, places, etc.) and one set for vocabulary words associated with the book.

WORD LIST
There is a word list for both the unit words and the vocabulary words. These lists show you which words are being used in the materials and the clues or definitions being used for those words. You may want to give students a word list with clues/definitions to help them, or you may want students to only have a word list (without clues/definitions) if you want them to work a little harder. Both are available for duplication. The word lists can also be your "calling key" for the bingo games.

FILL IN THE BLANK AND MATCHING
There are 4 each of the fill in the blank and matching worksheets for both the unit and vocabulary words. These pages can be used either as extra worksheets for students or as objective parts of a unit test. They can be done individually if students need extra help or as a whole class activity to review the material covered.

MAGIC SQUARES
The magic squares not only reinforce the material covered but also work on reasoning and math skills. Many teachers have told us that their students really enjoy doing these!

WORD SEARCH PUZZLES
The word search words go in all directions, as indicated on your answer keys. Two of the word search puzzles have the clues listed rather than the words. This makes the puzzle a little more difficult, but it reinforces the material better. Two word search puzzles have words only for students who find the clue puzzles too difficult.

CROSSWORD PUZZLES
Both unit and vocabulary word sections have 4 crossword puzzles.

BINGO CARDS
There are 32 individual bingo cards for the unit words and 32 individual bingo cards for the vocabulary words. You can use your word list as a "call list," calling the words at random and marking them off of your list as you go, or you could use the flash cards by cutting them apart and drawing the words at random from a hat (or box or whatever). To make a better review, you might ask for the definition and spelling of each word as you call it out–or you could call out the definitions and have students tell you the words they need to look for on the puzzle.

JUGGLE LETTERS
The vocabulary juggle letter game is intended to help students learn the spellings of the words. One sheet has the definitions listed on it as an extra help for students who need it or to reinforce the definitions if you choose to do so.

FLASH CARDS
We've included a set of vocabulary flash cards you can duplicate, cut, and fold for your students. Some teachers make a few sets for general use by the class; others make a set for each student. Some teachers duplicate them for each student and have the students cut & fold their own. You can cut out just the words and put them in a hat, have each student pick out one word and write the definition and a sentence for that word. Students then swap words and papers, with the next student adding a sentence of his own under the last one. You can have students swap as many times as you like. Each time the student will read the sentences written prior to his own and then add a sentence. You can cut out the words and definitions separately and play "I Have; Who Has?" Each student in the room draws a word and definition. The first student says, "I have (the name of the word). Who has the definition?" The student with the definition reads it then says, "I have (the name of the vocabulary word she has). Who has the definition?" The round continues until all words and definitions have been given.

The Pearl Word List

No.	Word	Clue/Definition
1.	BABY	Coyotito; for example
2.	BAD	Kind of luck the pearl brings Kino's family
3.	BID	Competitive offer to purchase something
4.	BUYERS	They fix the market and cheat the villagers
5.	CANOE	Symbol of tradition; the old way of life
6.	CAPITAL	Place Kino hopes to sell the pearl
7.	CONFLICT	Man vs. Society; for example
8.	COYOTITO	He is attacked by a scorpion
9.	DOCTOR	Refused to treat Coyotito at first
10.	EDUCATION	Kino's dream for Coyotito
11.	EVIL	Song of _____; a song of bad things
12.	FAMILY	Song of the _____; a song of happiness and harmony
13.	FISH	Symbolic of the natural way of the universe
14.	GOOD	_____ vs. Evil
15.	GULF	Final resting place of the pearl
16.	HAND	Kino injures his on the doctor's gate
17.	HARPOON	Fisherman's weapon Kino hopes to buy
18.	HUT	Kino's house; symbol of good and tradition
19.	INSTINCT	Animal intuition
20.	JUANA	Kino's wife
21.	KINO	He finds the pearl
22.	KNIFE	Kino's weapon against the intruder
23.	MAN	I am the _____
24.	MOUNTAIN	Place to which Kino, Juana and Coyotito flee
25.	NOVELLA	Short novel
26.	OMNISCIENT	A point of view
27.	OYSTER	Natural home of the pearl
28.	PATH	Place Kino is attacked and kills a man
29.	PEARL	Kino's find which holds his hopes for the future
30.	POULTICE	Seaweed pack on Coyotito's wound
31.	PRIEST	The pearl gave him ideas of church repairs
32.	SCORPION	It attacked Coyotito
33.	SONGS	Music in the story
34.	STEINBECK	Author
35.	TOMAS	Kino's brother; Juan ___
36.	TOWNSPEOPLE	They all think of the riches the pearl could bring them
37.	TRACKERS	One kills Coyotito; Kino kills them

The Pearl Fill In The Blank 1

_____

1. He finds the pearl
2. Music in the story
3. Kino's dream for Coyotito
4. Refused to treat Coyotito at first
5. Final resting place of the pearl
6. Kino's brother; Juan ___
7. Seaweed pack on Coyotito's wound
8. A point of view
9. Fisherman's weapon Kino hopes to buy
10. Competitive offer to purchase something
11. He is attacked by a scorpion
12. Kino's wife
13. They fix the market and cheat the villagers
14. Coyotito; for example
15. Kino's weapon against the intruder
16. One kills Coyotito; Kino kills them
17. Kino's house; symbol of good and tradition
18. Kino injures his on the doctor's gate
19. _____ vs. Evil
20. Natural home of the pearl

The Pearl Fill In The Blank 1 Answer Key

KINO	1. He finds the pearl
SONGS	2. Music in the story
EDUCATION	3. Kino's dream for Coyotito
DOCTOR	4. Refused to treat Coyotito at first
GULF	5. Final resting place of the pearl
TOMAS	6. Kino's brother; Juan ___
POULTICE	7. Seaweed pack on Coyotito's wound
OMNISCIENT	8. A point of view
HARPOON	9. Fisherman's weapon Kino hopes to buy
BID	10. Competitive offer to purchase something
COYOTITO	11. He is attacked by a scorpion
JUANA	12. Kino's wife
BUYERS	13. They fix the market and cheat the villagers
BABY	14. Coyotito; for example
KNIFE	15. Kino's weapon against the intruder
TRACKERS	16. One kills Coyotito; Kino kills them
HUT	17. Kino's house; symbol of good and tradition
HAND	18. Kino injures his on the doctor's gate
GOOD	19. _____ vs. Evil
OYSTER	20. Natural home of the pearl

The Pearl Fill In The Blank 2

_____

1. Competitive offer to purchase something
2. Short novel
3. Song of the _____, a song of happiness and harmony
4. Kino's dream for Coyotito
5. Place Kino is attacked and kills a man
6. Kino's wife
7. He is attacked by a scorpion
8. Kino's weapon against the intruder
9. Kino injures his on the doctor's gate
10. Man vs. Society; for example
11. Coyotito; for example
12. Seaweed pack on Coyotito's wound
13. Natural home of the pearl
14. Music in the story
15. He finds the pearl
16. It attacked Coyotito
17. They all think of the riches the pearl could bring them
18. A point of view
19. Symbolic of the natural way of the universe
20. Animal intuition

The Pearl Fill In The Blank 2 Answer Key

BID	1. Competitive offer to purchase something
NOVELLA	2. Short novel
FAMILY	3. Song of the _____, a song of happiness and harmony
EDUCATION	4. Kino's dream for Coyotito
PATH	5. Place Kino is attacked and kills a man
JUANA	6. Kino's wife
COYOTITO	7. He is attacked by a scorpion
KNIFE	8. Kino's weapon against the intruder
HAND	9. Kino injures his on the doctor's gate
CONFLICT	10. Man vs. Society; for example
BABY	11. Coyotito; for example
POULTICE	12. Seaweed pack on Coyotito's wound
OYSTER	13. Natural home of the pearl
SONGS	14. Music in the story
KINO	15. He finds the pearl
SCORPION	16. It attacked Coyotito
TOWNSPEOPLE	17. They all think of the riches the pearl could bring them
OMNISCIENT	18. A point of view
FISH	19. Symbolic of the natural way of the universe
INSTINCT	20. Animal intuition

The Pearl Fill In The Blank 3

_____

1. Kino's wife
2. Song of the _____; a song of happiness and harmony
3. Refused to treat Coyotito at first
4. He finds the pearl
5. A point of view
6. Kino's weapon against the intruder
7. Place to which Kino, Juana and Coyotito flee
8. Final resting place of the pearl
9. Place Kino is attacked and kills a man
10. Short novel
11. Kino injures his on the doctor's gate
12. I am the _____
13. It attacked Coyotito
14. Man vs. Society; for example
15. Kino's house; symbol of good and tradition
16. Song of _____; a song of bad things
17. Fisherman's weapon Kino hopes to buy
18. He is attacked by a scorpion
19. Coyotito, for example
20. Kino's find which holds his hopes for the future

The Pearl Fill In The Blank 3 Answer Key

JUANA	1. Kino's wife
FAMILY	2. Song of the _____; a song of happiness and harmony
DOCTOR	3. Refused to treat Coyotito at first
KINO	4. He finds the pearl
OMNISCIENT	5. A point of view
KNIFE	6. Kino's weapon against the intruder
MOUNTAIN	7. Place to which Kino, Juana and Coyotito flee
GULF	8. Final resting place of the pearl
PATH	9. Place Kino is attacked and kills a man
NOVELLA	10. Short novel
HAND	11. Kino injures his on the doctor's gate
MAN	12. I am the _____
SCORPION	13. It attacked Coyotito
CONFLICT	14. Man vs. Society; for example
HUT	15. Kino's house, symbol of good and tradition
EVIL	16. Song of _____; a song of bad things
HARPOON	17. Fisherman's weapon Kino hopes to buy
COYOTITO	18. He is attacked by a scorpion
BABY	19. Coyotito; for example
PEARL	20. Kino's find which holds his hopes for the future

The Pearl Fill In The Blank 4

_____

_____

_____

_____

_____

_____

_____

_____

_____

_____

_____

_____

_____

_____

_____

_____

_____

_____

_____

_____

1. One kills Coyotito; Kino kills them
2. Kino's brother; Juan ___
3. Song of the _____; a song of happiness and harmony
4. Natural home of the pearl
5. He is attacked by a scorpion
6. Song of _____; a song of bad things
7. Place to which Kino, Juana and Coyotito flee
8. Kino's dream for Coyotito
9. He finds the pearl
10. Competitive offer to purchase something
11. Fisherman's weapon Kino hopes to buy
12. Symbol of tradition; the old way of life
13. _____ vs. Evil
14. I am the _____
15. A point of view
16. Refused to treat Coyotito at first
17. Short novel
18. Kino's weapon against the intruder
19. Kind of luck the Pearl brings Kino's family
20. Kino's find which holds his hopes for the future

The Pearl Fill In The Blank 4 Answer Key

TRACKERS	1. One kills Coyotito; Kino kills them
TOMAS	2. Kino's brother; Juan ___
FAMILY	3. Song of the _____; a song of happiness and harmony
OYSTER	4. Natural home of the pearl
COYOTITO	5. He is attacked by a scorpion
EVIL	6. Song of _____; a song of bad things
MOUNTAIN	7. Place to which Kino, Juana and Coyotito flee
EDUCATION	8. Kino's dream for Coyotito
KINO	9. He finds the pearl
BID	10. Competitive offer to purchase something
HARPOON	11. Fisherman's weapon Kino hopes to buy
CANOE	12. Symbol of tradition; the old way of life
GOOD	13. _____ vs. Evil
MAN	14. I am the _____
OMNISCIENT	15. A point of view
DOCTOR	16. Refused to treat Coyotito at first
NOVELLA	17. Short novel
KNIFE	18. Kino's weapon against the intruder
BAD	19. Kind of luck the pearl brings Kino's family
PEARL	20. Kino's find which holds his hopes for the future

The Pearl Matching 1

___ 1. BID
___ 2. CANOE
___ 3. GOOD
___ 4. BUYERS
___ 5. KNIFE
___ 6. TOMAS
___ 7. STEINBECK
___ 8. PATH
___ 9. BAD
___ 10. EVIL
___ 11. GULF
___ 12. FAMILY
___ 13. BABY
___ 14. TOWNSPEOPLE
___ 15. INSTINCT
___ 16. POULTICE
___ 17. PRIEST
___ 18. DOCTOR
___ 19. HUT
___ 20. EDUCATION
___ 21. SONGS
___ 22. HARPOON
___ 23. JUANA
___ 24. OMNISCIENT
___ 25. SCORPION

A. Kino's house; symbol of good and tradition
B. Kino's wife
C. They all think of the riches the pearl could bring them
D. Symbol of tradition; the old way of life
E. Place Kino is attacked and kills a man
F. It attacked Coyotito
G. Animal intuition
H. A point of view
I. Author
J. Kino's weapon against the intruder
K. The pearl gave him ideas of church repairs
L. Competitive offer to purchase something
M. They fix the market and cheat the villagers
N. Kind of luck the pearl brings Kino's family
O. Seaweed pack on Coyotito's wound
P. Refused to treat Coyotito at first
Q. _____ vs. Evil
R. Kino's dream for Coyotito
S. Kino's brother; Juan ___
T. Coyotito; for example
U. Song of _____; a song of bad things
V. Fisherman's weapon Kino hopes to buy
W. Music in the story
X. Final resting place of the pearl
Y. Song of the _____; a song of happiness and harmony

The Pearl Matching 1 Answer Key

L - 1. BID	A.	Kino's house; symbol of good and tradition
D - 2. CANOE	B.	Kino's wife
Q - 3. GOOD	C.	They all think of the riches the pearl could bring them
M - 4. BUYERS	D.	Symbol of tradition; the old way of life
J - 5. KNIFE	E.	Place Kino is attacked and kills a man
S - 6. TOMAS	F.	It attacked Coyotito
I - 7. STEINBECK	G.	Animal intuition
E - 8. PATH	H.	A point of view
N - 9. BAD	I.	Author
U - 10. EVIL	J.	Kino's weapon against the intruder
X - 11. GULF	K.	The pearl gave him ideas of church repairs
Y - 12. FAMILY	L.	Competitive offer to purchase something
T - 13. BABY	M.	They fix the market and cheat the villagers
C - 14. TOWNSPEOPLE	N.	Kind of luck the pearl brings Kino's family
G - 15. INSTINCT	O.	Seaweed pack on Coyotito's wound
O - 16. POULTICE	P.	Refused to treat Coyotito at first
K - 17. PRIEST	Q.	_____ vs. Evil
P - 18. DOCTOR	R.	Kino's dream for Coyotito
A - 19. HUT	S.	Kino's brother; Juan ___
R - 20. EDUCATION	T.	Coyotito; for example
W - 21. SONGS	U.	Song of _____; a song of bad things
V - 22. HARPOON	V.	Fisherman's weapon Kino hopes to buy
B - 23. JUANA	W.	Music in the story
H - 24. OMNISCIENT	X.	Final resting place of the pearl
F - 25. SCORPION	Y.	Song of the _____; a song of happiness and harmony

The Pearl Matching 2

___ 1. OMNISCIENT
___ 2. NOVELLA
___ 3. EVIL
___ 4. SCORPION
___ 5. FISH
___ 6. HARPOON
___ 7. OYSTER
___ 8. HUT
___ 9. GULF
___ 10. DOCTOR
___ 11. JUANA
___ 12. KINO
___ 13. BID
___ 14. FAMILY
___ 15. GOOD
___ 16. TOMAS
___ 17. PEARL
___ 18. MOUNTAIN
___ 19. INSTINCT
___ 20. EDUCATION
___ 21. TRACKERS
___ 22. CANOE
___ 23. CAPITAL
___ 24. BABY
___ 25. BAD

A. Competitive offer to purchase something
B. Short novel
C. A point of view
D. It attacked Coyotito
E. Animal intuition
F. Kino's wife
G. Symbolic of the natural way of the universe
H. Coyotito; for example
I. Natural home of the pearl
J. Place to which Kino, Juana and Coyotito flee
K. Place Kino hopes to sell the pearl
L. Fisherman's weapon Kino hopes to buy
M. Refused to treat Coyotito at first
N. _____ vs. Evil
O. Kino's dream for Coyotito
P. Kino's find which holds his hopes for the future
Q. Final resting place of the pearl
R. Kino's brother; Juan ___
S. One kills Coyotito; Kino kills them
T. Song of _____; a song of bad things
U. Song of the _____; a song of happiness and harmony
V. Kino's house; symbol of good and tradition
W. Symbol of tradition; the old way of life
X. He finds the pearl
Y. Kind of luck the pearl brings Kino's family

The Pearl Matching 2 Answer Key

C - 1. OMNISCIENT	A. Competitive offer to purchase something
B - 2. NOVELLA	B. Short novel
T - 3. EVIL	C. A point of view
D - 4. SCORPION	D. It attacked Coyotito
G - 5. FISH	E. Animal intuition
L - 6. HARPOON	F. Kino's wife
I - 7. OYSTER	G. Symbolic of the natural way of the universe
V - 8. HUT	H. Coyotito; for example
Q - 9. GULF	I. Natural home of the pearl
M -10. DOCTOR	J. Place to which Kino, Juana and Coyotito flee
F -11. JUANA	K. Place Kino hopes to sell the pearl
X -12. KINO	L. Fisherman's weapon Kino hopes to buy
A -13. BID	M. Refused to treat Coyotito at first
U -14. FAMILY	N. _____ vs. Evil
N -15. GOOD	O. Kino's dream for Coyotito
R -16. TOMAS	P. Kino's find which holds his hopes for the future
P -17. PEARL	Q. Final resting place of the pearl
J -18. MOUNTAIN	R. Kino's brother; Juan ___
E -19. INSTINCT	S. One kills Coyotito; Kino kills them
O -20. EDUCATION	T. Song of _____; a song of bad things
S -21. TRACKERS	U. Song of the _____; a song of happiness and harmony
W -22. CANOE	V. Kino's house; symbol of good and tradition
K -23. CAPITAL	W. Symbol of tradition; the old way of life
H -24. BABY	X. He finds the pearl
Y -25. BAD	Y. Kind of luck the pearl brings Kino's family

Copyrighted

The Pearl Matching 3

___ 1. FISH A. Refused to treat Coyotito at first
___ 2. PATH B. Fisherman's weapon Kino hopes to buy
___ 3. TRACKERS C. Competitive offer to purchase something
___ 4. SCORPION D. Kino's house; symbol of good and tradition
___ 5. BAD E. Symbol of tradition; the old way of life
___ 6. NOVELLA F. Kino's wife
___ 7. KINO G. Animal intuition
___ 8. STEINBECK H. Place Kino is attacked and kills a man
___ 9. BUYERS I. Place Kino hopes to sell the pearl
___10. FAMILY J. _____ vs. Evil
___11. JUANA K. Short novel
___12. INSTINCT L. He finds the pearl
___13. BID M. He is attacked by a scorpion
___14. POULTICE N. Kino's brother; Juan ___
___15. CAPITAL O. Kind of luck the pearl brings Kino's family
___16. DOCTOR P. Song of the _____, a song of happiness and harmony
___17. TOMAS Q. One kills Coyotito; Kino kills them
___18. GOOD R. They fix the market and cheat the villagers
___19. EDUCATION S. They all think of the riches the pearl could bring them
___20. HARPOON T. Author
___21. CANOE U. Seaweed pack on Coyotito's wound
___22. TOWNSPEOPLE V. The pearl gave him ideas of church repairs
___23. PRIEST W. Symbolic of the natural way of the universe
___24. HUT X. It attacked Coyotito
___25. COYOTITO Y. Kino's dream for Coyotito

The Pearl Matching 3 Answer Key

W - 1. FISH	A. Refused to treat Coyotito at first
H - 2. PATH	B. Fisherman's weapon Kino hopes to buy
Q - 3. TRACKERS	C. Competitive offer to purchase something
X - 4. SCORPION	D. Kino's house; symbol of good and tradition
O - 5. BAD	E. Symbol of tradition; the old way of life
K - 6. NOVELLA	F. Kino's wife
L - 7. KINO	G. Animal intuition
T - 8. STEINBECK	H. Place Kino is attacked and kills a man
R - 9. BUYERS	I. Place Kino hopes to sell the pearl
P - 10. FAMILY	J. _____ vs. Evil
F - 11. JUANA	K. Short novel
G - 12. INSTINCT	L. He finds the pearl
C - 13. BID	M. He is attacked by a scorpion
U - 14. POULTICE	N. Kino's brother; Juan ___
I - 15. CAPITAL	O. Kind of luck the pearl brings Kino's family
A - 16. DOCTOR	P. Song of the _____; a song of happiness and harmony
N - 17. TOMAS	Q. One kills Coyotito; Kino kills them
J - 18. GOOD	R. They fix the market and cheat the villagers
Y - 19. EDUCATION	S. They all think of the riches the pearl could bring them
B - 20. HARPOON	T. Author
E - 21. CANOE	U. Seaweed pack on Coyotito's wound
S - 22. TOWNSPEOPLE	V. The pearl gave him ideas of church repairs
V - 23. PRIEST	W. Symbolic of the natural way of the universe
D - 24. HUT	X. It attacked Coyotito
M - 25. COYOTITO	Y. Kino's dream for Coyotito

The Pearl Matching 4

___ 1. SONGS   A. Kino's dream for Coyotito
___ 2. FAMILY   B. Place Kino is attacked and kills a man
___ 3. POULTICE   C. He finds the pearl
___ 4. KINO   D. It attacked Coyotito
___ 5. PATH   E. Man vs. Society; for example
___ 6. PEARL   F. Seaweed pack on Coyotito's wound
___ 7. FISH   G. Music in the story
___ 8. BAD   H. Kino's find which holds his hopes for the future
___ 9. BID   I. They fix the market and cheat the villagers
___ 10. MAN   J. Kino's wife
___ 11. DOCTOR   K. Refused to treat Coyotito at first
___ 12. OYSTER   L. Competitive offer to purchase something
___ 13. OMNISCIENT   M. I am the _____
___ 14. INSTINCT   N. Final resting place of the pearl
___ 15. SCORPION   O. Kind of luck the pearl brings Kino's family
___ 16. CONFLICT   P. Animal intuition
___ 17. HUT   Q. Author
___ 18. STEINBECK   R. Kino's weapon against the intruder
___ 19. TOMAS   S. A point of view
___ 20. MOUNTAIN   T. Natural home of the Pearl
___ 21. KNIFE   U. Symbolic of the natural way of the universe
___ 22. GULF   V. Place to which Kino, Juana and Coyotito flee
___ 23. BUYERS   W. Song of the _____; a song of happiness and harmony
___ 24. JUANA   X. Kino's house; symbol of good and tradition
___ 25. EDUCATION   Y. Kino's brother; Juan ___

The Pearl Matching 4 Answer Key

G - 1. SONGS	A.	Kino's dream for Coyotito
W - 2. FAMILY	B.	Place Kino is attacked and kills a man
F - 3. POULTICE	C.	He finds the pearl
C - 4. KINO	D.	It attacked Coyotito
B - 5. PATH	E.	Man vs. Society; for example
H - 6. PEARL	F.	Seaweed pack on Coyotito's wound
U - 7. FISH	G.	Music in the story
O - 8. BAD	H.	Kino's find which holds his hopes for the future
L - 9. BID	I.	They fix the market and cheat the villagers
M -10. MAN	J.	Kino's wife
K -11. DOCTOR	K.	Refused to treat Coyotito at first
T -12. OYSTER	L.	Competitive offer to purchase something
S -13. OMNISCIENT	M.	I am the _____
P -14. INSTINCT	N.	Final resting place of the pearl
D -15. SCORPION	O.	Kind of luck the pearl brings Kino's family
E -16. CONFLICT	P.	Animal intuition
X -17. HUT	Q.	Author
Q -18. STEINBECK	R.	Kino's weapon against the intruder
Y -19. TOMAS	S.	A point of view
V -20. MOUNTAIN	T.	Natural home of the pearl
R -21. KNIFE	U.	Symbolic of the natural way of the universe
N -22. GULF	V.	Place to which Kino, Juana and Coyotito flee
I - 23. BUYERS	W.	Song of the _____; a song of happiness and harmony
J - 24. JUANA	X.	Kino's house; symbol of good and tradition
A -25. EDUCATION	Y.	Kino's brother; Juan ___

The Pearl Magic Squares 1

Match the definition with the vocabulary word. Put your answers in the magic squares below. When your answers are correct, all columns and rows will add to the same number.

A. OYSTER
B. BID
C. TOWNSPEOPLE
D. PEARL
E. KNIFE
F. KINO
G. STEINBECK
H. POULTICE
I. CANOE
J. NOVELLA
K. MOUNTAIN
L. BABY
M. EDUCATION
N. FISH
O. TOMAS
P. INSTINCT

1. Kino's brother; Juan ___
2. Short novel
3. Seaweed pack on Coyotito's wound
4. Natural home of the pearl
5. Kino's find which holds his hopes for the future
6. Kino's weapon against the intruder
7. Place to which Kino, Juana and Coyotito flee
8. Symbolic of the natural way of the universe
9. He finds the pearl
10. They all think of the riches the pearl could bring them
11. Kino's dream for Coyotito
12. Coyotito; for example
13. Symbol of tradition; the old way of life
14. Animal intuition
15. Competitive offer to purchase something
16. Author

A= 4	B= 15	C= 10	D= 5
E= 6	F= 9	G= 16	H= 3
I= 13	J= 2	K= 7	L= 12
M= 11	N= 8	O= 1	P= 14

The Pearl Magic Squares 1 Answer Key

Match the definition with the vocabulary word. Put your answers in the magic squares below. When your answers are correct, all columns and rows will add to the same number.

A. OYSTER
B. BID
C. TOWNSPEOPLE
D. PEARL
E. KNIFE
F. KINO
G. STEINBECK
H. POULTICE
I. CANOE
J. NOVELLA
K. MOUNTAIN
L. BABY
M. EDUCATION
N. FISH
O. TOMAS
P. INSTINCT

1. Kino's brother; Juan ___
2. Short novel
3. Seaweed pack on Coyotito's wound
4. Natural home of the pearl
5. Kino's find which holds his hopes for the future
6. Kino's weapon against the intruder
7. Place to which Kino, Juana and Coyotito flee
8. Symbolic of the natural way of the universe
9. He finds the pearl
10. They all think of the riches the pearl could bring them
11. Kino's dream for Coyotito
12. Coyotito; for example
13. Symbol of tradition; the old way of life
14. Animal intuition
15. Competitive offer to purchase something
16. Author

A=4	B=15	C=10	D=5
E=6	F=9	G=16	H=3
I=13	J=2	K=7	L=12
M=11	N=8	O=1	P=14

The Pearl Magic Squares 2

Match the definition with the vocabulary word. Put your answers in the magic squares below. When your answers are correct, all columns and rows will add to the same number.

A. BAD
B. BUYERS
C. PEARL
D. PATH
E. HAND
F. GULF
G. DOCTOR
H. FAMILY
I. EVIL
J. BID
K. OMNISCIENT
L. NOVELLA
M. EDUCATION
N. OYSTER
O. MAN
P. INSTINCT

1. They fix the market and cheat the villagers
2. Refused to treat Coyotito at first
3. A point of view
4. Natural home of the pearl
5. Kino's dream for Coyotito
6. Short novel
7. Song of _____; a song of happiness and harmony
8. Kind of luck the pearl brings Kino's family
9. Animal intuition
10. Song of _____; a song of bad things
11. Kino injures his on the doctor's gate
12. Place Kino is attacked and kills a man
13. Kino's find which holds his hopes for the future
14. Final resting place of the pearl
15. Competitive offer to purchase something
16. I am the _____

A=	B=	C=	D=
E=	F=	G=	H=
I=	J=	K=	L=
M=	N=	O=	P=

The Pearl Magic Squares 2 Answer Key

Match the definition with the vocabulary word. Put your answers in the magic squares below. When your answers are correct, all columns and rows will add to the same number.

A. BAD
B. BUYERS
C. PEARL
D. PATH
E. HAND
F. GULF
G. DOCTOR
H. FAMILY
I. EVIL
J. BID
K. OMNISCIENT
L. NOVELLA
M. EDUCATION
N. OYSTER
O. MAN
P. INSTINCT

1. They fix the market and cheat the villagers
2. Refused to treat Coyotito at first
3. A point of view
4. Natural home of the pearl
5. Kino's dream for Coyotito
6. Short novel
7. Song of _____; a song of happiness and harmony
8. Kind of luck the pearl brings Kino's family
9. Animal intuition
10. Song of _____; a song of bad things
11. Kino injures his on the doctor's gate
12. Place Kino is attacked and kills a man
13. Kino's find which holds his hopes for the future
14. Final resting place of the pearl
15. Competitive offer to purchase something
16. I am the _____

A=8	B=1	C=13	D=12
E=11	F=14	G=2	H=7
I=10	J=15	K=3	L=6
M=5	N=4	O=16	P=9

The Pearl Magic Squares 3

Match the definition with the vocabulary word. Put your answers in the magic squares below. When your answers are correct, all columns and rows will add to the same number.

A. MAN
B. STEINBECK
C. NOVELLA
D. BUYERS
E. CANOE
F. TRACKERS
G. BID
H. OMNISCIENT
I. EDUCATION
J. HARPOON
K. BABY
L. SONGS
M. CONFLICT
N. EVIL
O. GULF
P. INSTINCT

1. Short novel
2. Fisherman's weapon Kino hopes to buy
3. One kills Coyotito; Kino kills them
4. Final resting place of the pearl
5. Animal intuition
6. Symbol of tradition; the old way of life
7. Kino's dream for Coyotito
8. They fix the market and cheat the villagers
9. Man vs. Society; for example
10. A point of view
11. Music in the story
12. I am the _____
13. Author
14. Coyotito; for example
15. Competitive offer to purchase something
16. Song of _____; a song of bad things

A= 12	B= 13	C= 1	D= 8
E= 6	F= 3	G= 15	H= 10
I= 7	J= 2	K= 14	L= 11
M= 9	N= 16	O= 4	P= 5

The Pearl Magic Squares 3 Answer Key

Match the definition with the vocabulary word. Put your answers in the magic squares below. When your answers are correct, all columns and rows will add to the same number.

A. MAN
B. STEINBECK
C. NOVELLA
D. BUYERS
E. CANOE
F. TRACKERS
G. BID
H. OMNISCIENT
I. EDUCATION
J. HARPOON
K. BABY
L. SONGS
M. CONFLICT
N. EVIL
O. GULF
P. INSTINCT

1. Short novel
2. Fisherman's weapon Kino hopes to buy
3. One kills Coyotito; Kino kills them
4. Final resting place of the pearl
5. Animal intuition
6. Symbol of tradition; the old way of life
7. Kino's dream for Coyotito
8. They fix the market and cheat the villagers
9. Man vs. Society; for example
10. A point of view
11. Music in the story
12. I am the _____
13. Author
14. Coyotito; for example
15. Competitive offer to purchase something
16. Song of _____; a song of bad things

A=12	B=13	C=1	D=8
E=6	F=3	G=15	H=10
I=7	J=2	K=14	L=11
M=9	N=16	O=4	P=5

The Pearl Magic Squares 4

Match the definition with the vocabulary word. Put your answers in the magic squares below. When your answers are correct, all columns and rows will add to the same number.

A. BUYERS
B. OMNISCIENT
C. PEARL
D. HAND
E. EDUCATION
F. GULF
G. PATH
H. PRIEST
I. MAN
J. TOWNSPEOPLE
K. SONGS
L. TRACKERS
M. FAMILY
N. CANOE
O. NOVELLA
P. COYOTITO

1. The pearl gave him ideas of church repairs
2. Song of the _____; a song of happiness and harmony
3. A point of view
4. Music in the story
5. They all think of the riches the pearl could bring them
6. Kino's find which holds his hopes for the future
7. He is attacked by a scorpion
8. Kino's dream for Coyotito
9. Short novel
10. Final resting place of the pearl
11. I am the _____
12. Kino injures his on the doctor's gate
13. They fix the market and cheat the villagers
14. One kills Coyotito; Kino kills them
15. Place Kino is attacked and kills a man
16. Symbol of tradition; the old way of life

A=	B=	C=	D=
E=	F=	G=	H=
I=	J=	K=	L=
M=	N=	O=	P=

The Pearl Magic Squares 4 Answer Key

Match the definition with the vocabulary word. Put your answers in the magic squares below. When your answers are correct, all columns and rows will add to the same number.

A. BUYERS
B. OMNISCIENT
C. PEARL
D. HAND
E. EDUCATION
F. GULF
G. PATH
H. PRIEST
I. MAN
J. TOWNSPEOPLE
K. SONGS
L. TRACKERS
M. FAMILY
N. CANOE
O. NOVELLA
P. COYOTITO

1. The pearl gave him ideas of church repairs
2. Song of the _____; a song of happiness and harmony
3. A point of view
4. Music in the story
5. They all think of the riches the pearl could bring them
6. Kino's find which holds his hopes for the future
7. He is attacked by a scorpion
8. Kino's dream for Coyotito
9. Short novel
10. Final resting place of the pearl
11. I am the _____
12. Kino injures his on the doctor's gate
13. They fix the market and cheat the villagers
14. One kills Coyotito; Kino kills them
15. Place Kino is attacked and kills a man
16. Symbol of tradition; the old way of life

A=13	B=3	C=6	D=12
E=8	F=10	G=15	H=1
I=11	J=5	K=4	L=14
M=2	N=16	O=9	P=7

The Pearl Word Search 1

Words are placed backwards, forward, diagonally, up and down. Clues listed below can help you find the words. Circle the hidden vocabulary words in the maze.

```
J U A N A X P E A R L D A B P H H B
V B B A M P O J D A H Z K I A A U G
N X U M R N M L T U B A P D T R T R
Q G Y I A H Y I X D C A N Y H P D Y
S V E C W C P G U L F A B D T O O P
V S R H S A O M G N I A T Y V O C H
T S S T C B S N F E S M M I K N T W
E V I L O H H O F Z H C S I O R O C
J T M G R W H I N L K R A G L N R C
P B V Q P C N M S G I Z M O I Y M G
B O F C I K O S C X S C O O N I K B
G Q U C O U N X P R X D T D S H F H
C V N L N Y S O E E N O Y S T E R T
P Z Y T T R O K V G O R X L I Y K X
D Z A F B I C T R E N P W R N S Y N
V I M K R A C F I T L C L B C D V C
N H S V R P Y E S T R L G E T B N J
B Q F T R Y L P D Q O G A W K N D Y
```

Animal intuition (8)
Competitive offer to purchase something (3)
Coyotito; for example (4)
Final resting place of the pearl (4)
Fisherman's weapon Kino hopes to buy (7)
He finds the pearl (4)
He is attacked by a scorpion (8)
I am the _____ (3)
It attacked Coyotito (8)
Kind of luck the pearl brings Kino's family (3)
Kino injures his ___ on the doctor's gate (4)
Kino's brother; Juan ___ (5)
Kino's dream for Coyotito (9)
Kino's find which holds his hopes for the future (5)
Kino's house, symbol of good and tradition (3)
Kino's weapon against the intruder (5)
Kino's wife (5)
Man vs. Society; for example (8)
Music in the story (5)
Natural home of the pearl (6)
One kills Coyotito; Kino kills them (8)
Place Kino hopes to sell the pearl (7)
Place Kino is attacked and kills a man (4)
Place to which Kino, Juana and Coyotito flee (8)
Refused to treat Coyotito at first (6)
Seaweed pack on Coyotito's wound (8)
Short novel (7)
Song of _____; a song of bad things (4)
Song of the _____; a song of happiness and harmony (6)
Symbol of tradition; the old way of life (5)
Symbolic of the natural way of the universe (4)
The pearl gave him ideas of church repairs (6)
They all think of the riches the pearl could bring them (11)
They fix the market and cheat the villagers (6)
_____ vs. Evil (4)

The Pearl Word Search 1 Answer Key

Words are placed backwards, forward, diagonally, up and down. Clues listed below can help you find the words. Circle the hidden vocabulary words in the maze.

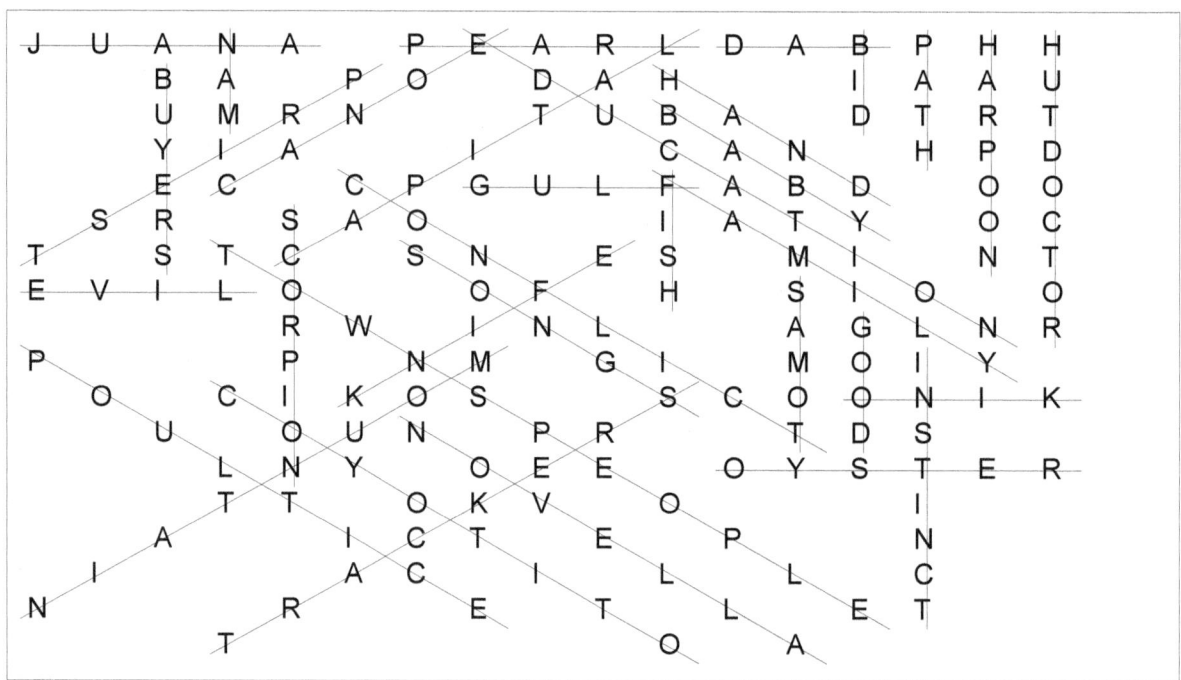

Animal intuition (8)
Competitive offer to purchase something (3)
Coyotito; for example (4)
Final resting place of the pearl (4)
Fisherman's weapon Kino hopes to buy (7)
He finds the pearl (4)
He is attacked by a scorpion (8)
I am the _____ (3)
It attacked Coyotito (8)
Kind of luck the pearl brings Kino's family (3)
Kino injures his on the doctor's gate (4)
Kino's brother; Juan ___ (5)
Kino's dream for Coyotito (9)
Kino's find which holds his hopes for the future (5)
Kino's house, symbol of good and tradition (3)
Kino's weapon against the intruder (5)
Kino's wife (5)
Man vs. Society; for example (8)
Music in the story (5)
Natural home of the pearl (6)

One kills Coyotito; Kino kills them (8)
Place Kino hopes to sell the pearl (7)
Place Kino is attacked and kills a man (4)
Place to which Kino, Juana and Coyotito flee (8)
Refused to treat Coyotito at first (6)
Seaweed pack on Coyotito's wound (8)
Short novel (7)
Song of _____; a song of bad things (4)
Song of the _____; a song of happiness and harmony (6)
Symbol of tradition; the old way of life (5)
Symbolic of the natural way of the universe (4)
The pearl gave him ideas of church repairs (6)
They all think of the riches the pearl could bring them (11)
They fix the market and cheat the villagers (6)
_____ vs. Evil (4)

The Pearl Word Search 2

Words are placed backwards, forward, diagonally, up and down. Clues listed below can help you find the words. Circle the hidden vocabulary words in the maze.

```
P O Y S T E R G U L F H F T A K D Y
A E Z V B R T H D B R W A N O I J B
T N A F V A A X T P X D A R B M G K
H N G R W G B C K C W U C J P M A G
N O V E L L A Y K S J E A W Q O T S
W I G T V S K Y G E C K P F T T O S
L T R H R W L N X I R K I I P S W N
T A Q E R G O T T R J S T P Z T N J
Y C Y Y C S C L S V C O A K T V S Q
D U F F V N U T R N Y S L V Z N P Z
B D V J I O G V T O T X M L T O E P
D E B T P L D C C X J N Y C C I O B
Y T S E P P I Z D D P W M A K P P Z
L N D F B L E Z F O R X N D M R L S
I M Y I F J V K I C I O D A J O E F
M O U N T A I N S T E I N B E C K V
A L O K W N L M H O S V A H K S X D
F C G O O D S W R R T R H H U T J N
```

Animal intuition (8)
Author (9)
Competitive offer to purchase something (3)
Coyotito; for example (4)
Final resting place of the pearl (4)
Fisherman's weapon Kino hopes to buy (7)
He finds the pearl (4)
He is attacked by a scorpion (8)
I am the _____ (3)
It attacked Coyotito (8)
Kind of luck the pearl brings Kino's family (3)
Kino injures his on the doctor's gate (4)
Kino's brother; Juan ___ (5)
Kino's dream for Coyotito (9)
Kino's find which holds his hopes for the future (5)
Kino's house; symbol of good and tradition (3)
Kino's weapon against the intruder (5)
Kino's wife (5)
Man vs. Society; for example (8)
Music in the story (5)

Natural home of the pearl (6)
One kills Coyotito; Kino kills them (8)
Place Kino hopes to sell the pearl (7)
Place Kino is attacked and kills a man (4)
Place to which Kino, Juana and Coyotito flee (8)
Refused to treat Coyotito at first (6)
Seaweed pack on Coyotito's wound (8)
Short novel (7)
Song of _____; a song of bad things (4)
Song of the _____; a song of happiness and harmony (6)
Symbol of tradition; the old way of life (5)
Symbolic of the natural way of the universe (4)
The pearl gave him ideas of church repairs (6)
They all think of the riches the pearl could bring them (11)
They fix the market and cheat the villagers (6)
_____ vs. Evil (4)

The Pearl Word Search 2 Answer Key

Words are placed backwards, forward, diagonally, up and down. Clues listed below can help you find the words. Circle the hidden vocabulary words in the maze.

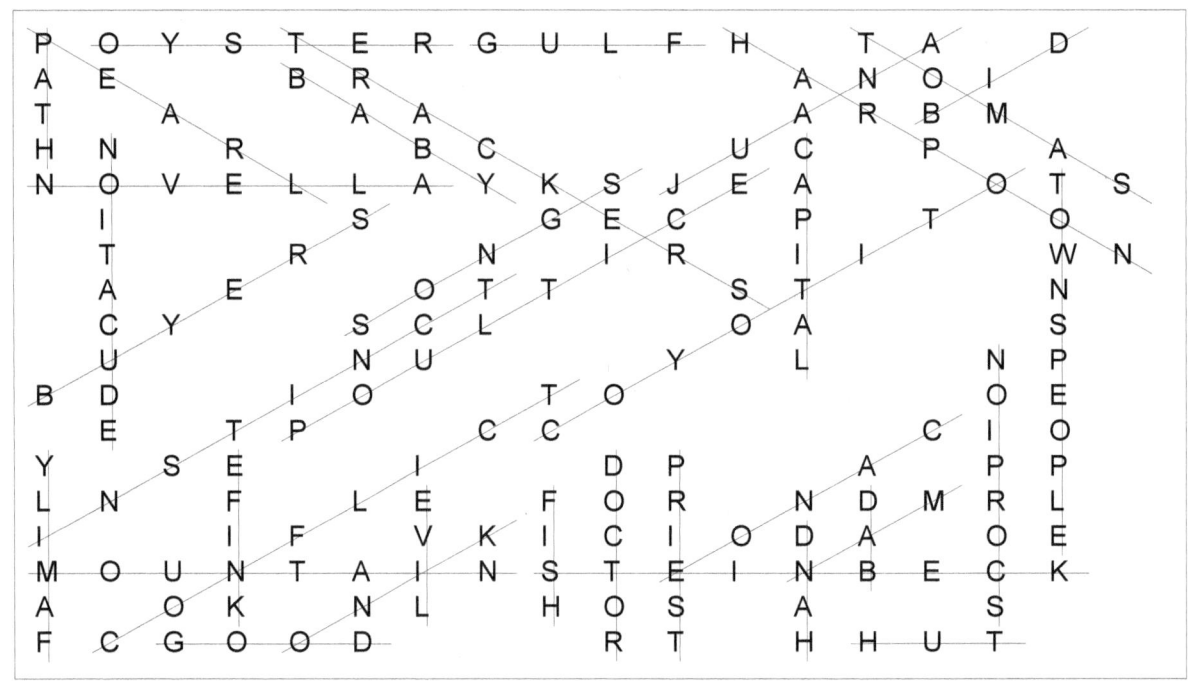

Animal intuition (8)
Author (9)
Competitive offer to purchase something (3)
Coyotito; for example (4)
Final resting place of the pearl (4)
Fisherman's weapon Kino hopes to buy (7)
He finds the pearl (4)
He is attacked by a scorpion (8)
I am the _____ (3)
It attacked Coyotito (8)
Kind of luck the pearl brings Kino's family (3)
Kino injures his on the doctor's gate (4)
Kino's brother; Juan ___ (5)
Kino's dream for Coyotito (9)
Kino's find which holds his hopes for the future (5)
Kino's house; symbol of good and tradition (3)
Kino's weapon against the intruder (5)
Kino's wife (5)
Man vs. Society; for example (8)
Music in the story (5)

Natural home of the pearl (6)
One kills Coyotito; Kino kills them (8)
Place Kino hopes to sell the pearl (7)
Place Kino is attacked and kills a man (4)
Place to which Kino, Juana and Coyotito flee (8)
Refused to treat Coyotito at first (6)
Seaweed pack on Coyotito's wound (8)
Short novel (7)
Song of _____; a song of bad things (4)
Song of the _____; a song of happiness and harmony (6)
Symbol of tradition; the old way of life (5)
Symbolic of the natural way of the universe (4)
The pearl gave him ideas of church repairs (6)
They all think of the riches the pearl could bring them (11)
They fix the market and cheat the villagers (6)
_____ vs. Evil (4)

The Pearl Word Search 3

Words are placed backwards, forward, diagonally, up and down. Words listed below are included in the maze. Circle the hidden vocabulary words in the maze.

```
P V C S P F N J G D S Y R P F C V E J D
R B A T N E I C S I N M O B A B Y V U P
L K P E O B A S D G G H A N M C B I A T
K Z I I T W T Z H N M D O N I L C L N Q
T G T N O Y N C F V P E F Y L O R H A L
B P A B M M U S P E A R L N Y P Z X S J
C I L E A H O D P Z B G I O B X R R C V
G Q D C S N M B D E B K T E X Q E O O S
X U B K G H O Z L N O I P B S Y K T R Y
G J L S F Q U V F J T P J N U T P C P B
K H K F D Y K T E O Y V L B T B A O I L
B I Y Y F D K Q R L G J T E R K T D O W
W V N O O P R A H M L N D N A H H G N B
V J C O N V M L X F G A X Z C G P Z X C
Y N L N Q H Y R S G X R K S K W O G T Z
E D U C A T I O N D K N I F E H S O W N
F B D J Y J M P A M W L W Q R P K F D P
R G H D N Z R B P F R F I N S T I N C T
P O U L T I C E K N T G G J B N K Q V M
C O N F L I C T O Y S T E R D B T F J N
```

BABY	GOOD	OYSTER
BAD	GULF	PATH
BID	HAND	PEARL
BUYERS	HARPOON	POULTICE
CANOE	HUT	PRIEST
CAPITAL	INSTINCT	SCORPION
CONFLICT	JUANA	SONGS
COYOTITO	KINO	STEINBECK
DOCTOR	KNIFE	TOMAS
EDUCATION	MAN	TOWNSPEOPLE
EVIL	MOUNTAIN	TRACKERS
FAMILY	NOVELLA	
FISH	OMNISCIENT	

The Pearl Word Search 3 Answer Key

Words are placed backwards, forward, diagonally, up and down. Words listed below are included in the maze. Circle the hidden vocabulary words in the maze.

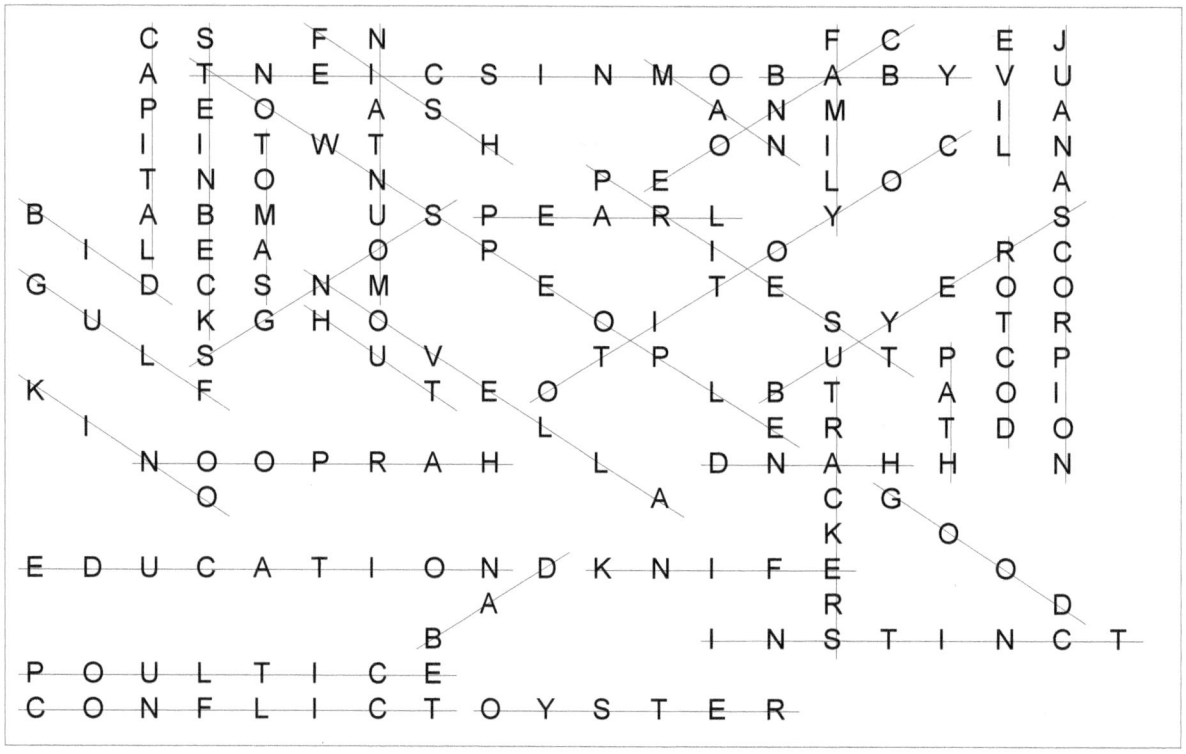

BABY	GOOD	OYSTER
BAD	GULF	PATH
BID	HAND	PEARL
BUYERS	HARPOON	POULTICE
CANOE	HUT	PRIEST
CAPITAL	INSTINCT	SCORPION
CONFLICT	JUANA	SONGS
COYOTITO	KINO	STEINBECK
DOCTOR	KNIFE	TOMAS
EDUCATION	MAN	TOWNSPEOPLE
EVIL	MOUNTAIN	TRACKERS
FAMILY	NOVELLA	
FISH	OMNISCIENT	

The Pearl Word Search 4

Words are placed backwards, forward, diagonally, up and down. Words listed below are included in the maze. Circle the hidden vocabulary words in the maze.

```
E D U C A T I O N F T N O V E L L A K R
D V K H S Q Y M I I O R H D F M V Z I C
T Q I D T S R N A S W S A W I L W H N B
C B N L T K J I T H N T C C N J P P O W
J A T E C Q G S N P S E Q A K D E B B H
H G R F H R N C U O P I N P C E A D A V
F Z L D F S J I O U E N F I O S R L B J
X U Z H O N B E M L O B Z T Y O L S Y Y
G V L B D C K N H T P E H A O N V P R B
H M C N J S T T S I L C S L T G C C I H
Z Z R C X W D O N C E K J X I S Z W N L
C O N F L I C T R E M M T T H H F S S
G N J M F Z V Q M V F M Z S O L P A T R
G S C N R M Y F S W S B Q E M L N M I P
C M V N X S Y Q Y R J H F I S O M I N H
K L M N Y D S G J H R E K R O D N L C B
N Q W D L S S H U S C O R P I O N Y T R
Z B O H V B T N A P D N R G P C K U T D
G O I V A A X A N B G A T F C T H P X L
G S G D P T O M A S H C B U Y E R S V B
```

BABY	GOOD	OYSTER
BAD	GULF	PATH
BID	HAND	PEARL
BUYERS	HARPOON	POULTICE
CANOE	HUT	PRIEST
CAPITAL	INSTINCT	SCORPION
CONFLICT	JUANA	SONGS
COYOTITO	KINO	STEINBECK
DOCTOR	KNIFE	TOMAS
EDUCATION	MAN	TOWNSPEOPLE
EVIL	MOUNTAIN	TRACKERS
FAMILY	NOVELLA	
FISH	OMNISCIENT	

The Pearl Word Search 4 Answer Key

Words are placed backwards, forward, diagonally, up and down. Words listed below are included in the maze. Circle the hidden vocabulary words in the maze.

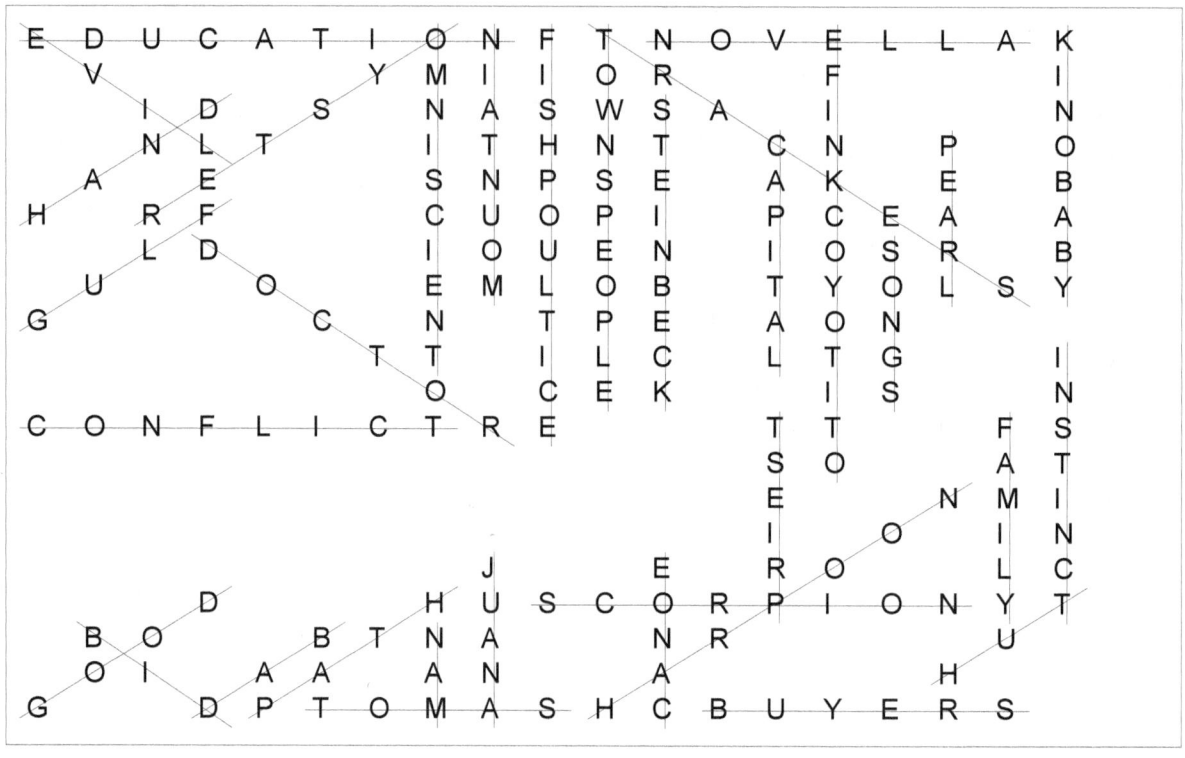

BABY	GOOD	OYSTER
BAD	GULF	PATH
BID	HAND	PEARL
BUYERS	HARPOON	POULTICE
CANOE	HUT	PRIEST
CAPITAL	INSTINCT	SCORPION
CONFLICT	JUANA	SONGS
COYOTITO	KINO	STEINBECK
DOCTOR	KNIFE	TOMAS
EDUCATION	MAN	TOWNSPEOPLE
EVIL	MOUNTAIN	TRACKERS
FAMILY	NOVELLA	
FISH	OMNISCIENT	

The Pearl Crossword 1

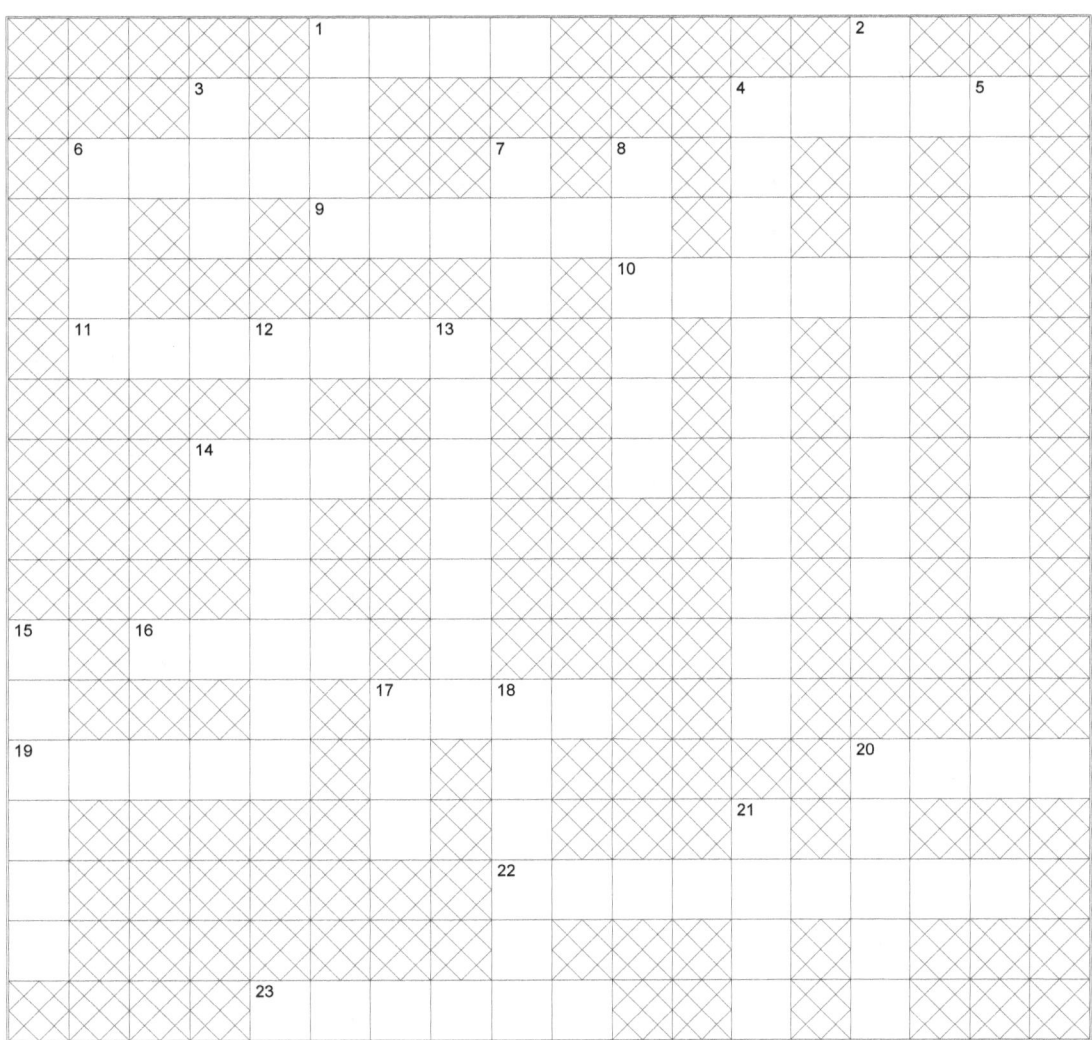

Across
1. _____ vs. Evil
4. Kino's brother; Juan ___
6. Kino's find which holds his hopes for the future
9. Song of the _____; a song of happiness and harmony
10. Music in the story
11. Fisherman's weapon Kino hopes to buy
14. Kino's house; symbol of good and tradition
16. Song of _____; a song of bad things
17. Coyotito; for example
19. Symbol of tradition; the old way of life
20. He finds the pearl
22. Kino's dream for Coyotito
23. The pearl gave him ideas of church repairs

Down
1. Final resting place of the pearl
2. A point of view
3. I am the _____
4. They all think of the riches the pearl could bring them
5. Author
6. Place Kino is attacked and kills a man
7. Competitive offer to purchase something
8. Natural home of the pearl
12. Seaweed pack on Coyotito's wound
13. Short novel
15. Refused to treat Coyotito at first
17. Kind of luck the pearl brings Kino's family
18. They fix the market and cheat the villagers
20. Kino's weapon against the intruder
21. Kino injures his on the doctor's gate

The Pearl Crossword 1 Answer Key

				1 G	O	O	D					2 O	
		3 M		U						4 T	O	M	A	5 S
	6 P	E	A	R	L		7 B		8 O		O		N		T
		A		N		9 F	A	M	I	L	Y		W		I	E
		T					D		10 S	O	N	G	S		I
	11 H	A	R	12 P	O	O	13 N		T		S		C		N	B
				O			O		E		P		I		B
			14 H	U	T		V		R		E		E		E
				L			E				O		N		C
				T			L				P		T		K
15 D		16 E	V	I	L		L				L		
O				C		17 B	18 A	Y			E	
19 C	A	N	O	E		A	U					20 K	I	N	O
T						D	Y				21 H	N
O						22 E	D	U	C	A	T	I	O	N
R						R					N	F
			23 P	R	I	E	S	T		D	E

Across
1. _____ vs. Evil
4. Kino's brother; Juan ___
6. Kino's find which holds his hopes for the future
9. Song of the _____; a song of happiness and harmony
10. Music in the story
11. Fisherman's weapon Kino hopes to buy
14. Kino's house; symbol of good and tradition
16. Song of _____; a song of bad things
17. Coyotito; for example
19. Symbol of tradition; the old way of life
20. He finds the pearl
22. Kino's dream for Coyotito
23. The pearl gave him ideas of church repairs

Down
1. Final resting place of the pearl
2. A point of view
3. I am the _____
4. They all think of the riches the pearl could bring them
5. Author
6. Place Kino is attacked and kills a man
7. Competitive offer to purchase something
8. Natural home of the pearl
12. Seaweed pack on Coyotito's wound
13. Short novel
15. Refused to treat Coyotito at first
17. Kind of luck the pearl brings Kino's family
18. They fix the market and cheat the villagers
20. Kino's weapon against the intruder
21. Kino injures his on the doctor's gate

The Pearl Crossword 2

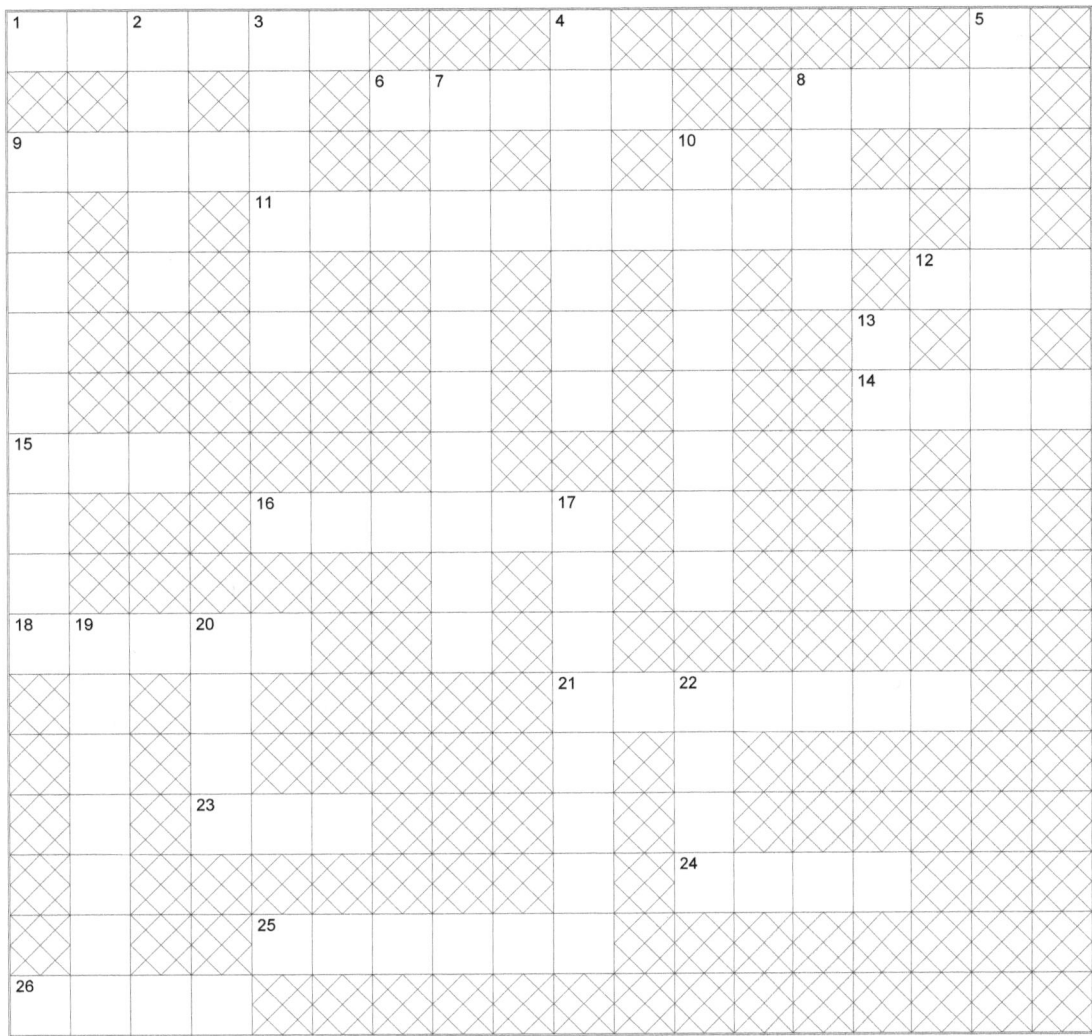

Across
1. Refused to treat Coyotito at first
6. Kino's brother; Juan ___
8. _____ vs. Evil
9. Music in the story
11. They all think of the riches the pearl could bring them
12. Kind of luck the Pearl brings Kino's family
14. Song of _____; a song of bad things
15. Competitive offer to purchase something
16. The pearl gave him ideas of church repairs
18. Kino's weapon against the intruder
21. Place Kino hopes to sell the pearl
23. Kino's house; symbol of good and tradition
24. Kino injures his on the doctor's gate
25. They fix the market and cheat the villagers
26. Coyotito; for example

Down
2. Symbol of tradition; the old way of life
3. Natural home of the pearl
4. Fisherman's weapon Kino hopes to buy
5. Kino's dream for Coyotito
7. A point of view
8. Final resting place of the pearl
9. Author
10. Seaweed pack on Coyotito's wound
13. Kino's find which holds his hopes for the future
17. One kills Coyotito; Kino kills them
19. Short novel
20. Symbolic of the natural way of the universe
22. Place Kino is attacked and kills a man

The Pearl Crossword 2 Answer Key

	1 D	2 O	3 C	T	O	R			4 H					5 E
		A		Y		6 T	7 O	M	A	S		8 G	O	O	D
	9 S	O	N	G	S		M		R		10 P	U		U
	T		11 T	O	W	N	S	P	E	O	P	L	E	12 B	A	D
	E		E			I		O		U		F	13 P	A	T
	I		R			S		O		L			14 E	V	I	L
	N					C		N		T			A		O
	15 B	I	D			I				I			A		O
	E		16 P	R	I	E	S	17 T		C			R		N
	C					N		R		E			L
	18 K	19 N	20 F	E			T		A
		O	I					21 C	22 A	P	I	T	A	L
		V	S					K		A
		E	23 H	U	T			E		T
		L						R		24 H	A	N	D
		L	25 B	U	Y	E	R	S
	26 B	A	B	Y

Across
1. Refused to treat Coyotito at first
6. Kino's brother; Juan ___
8. _____ vs. Evil
9. Music in the story
11. They all think of the riches the pearl could bring them
12. Kind of luck the Pearl brings Kino's family
14. Song of _____; a song of bad things
15. Competitive offer to purchase something
16. The pearl gave him ideas of church repairs
18. Kino's weapon against the intruder
21. Place Kino hopes to sell the pearl
23. Kino's house; symbol of good and tradition
24. Kino injures his on the doctor's gate
25. They fix the market and cheat the villagers
26. Coyotito; for example

Down
2. Symbol of tradition; the old way of life
3. Natural home of the pearl
4. Fisherman's weapon Kino hopes to buy
5. Kino's dream for Coyotito
7. A point of view
8. Final resting place of the pearl
9. Author
10. Seaweed pack on Coyotito's wound
13. Kino's find which holds his hopes for the future
17. One kills Coyotito; Kino kills them
19. Short novel
20. Symbolic of the natural way of the universe
22. Place Kino is attacked and kills a man

The Pearl Crossword 3

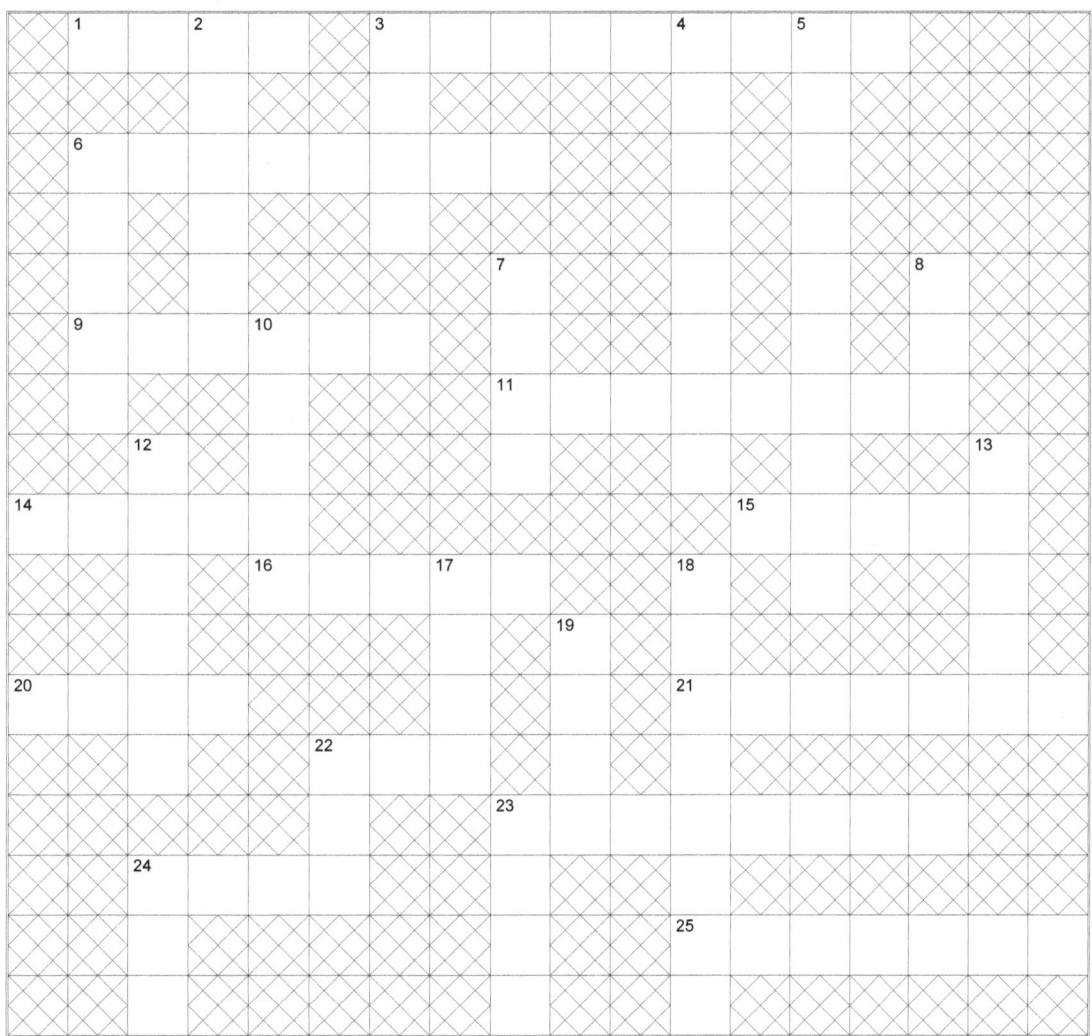

Across
1. Coyotito; for example
3. Kino's dream for Coyotito
6. He is attacked by a scorpion
9. Natural home of the pearl
11. It attacked Coyotito
14. Kino's wife
15. Kino's weapon against the intruder
16. Music in the story
20. Final resting place of the pearl
21. Short novel
22. Competitive offer to purchase something
23. Seaweed pack on Coyotito's wound
24. Kino injures his on the doctor's gate
25. Place Kino hopes to sell the pearl

Down
2. They fix the market and cheat the villagers
3. Song of _____; a song of bad things
4. One kills Coyotito; Kino kills them
5. A point of view
6. Symbol of tradition, the old way of life
7. Symbolic of the natural way of the universe
8. I am the _____
10. Kino's brother; Juan ___
12. Song of the _____; a song of happiness and harmony
13. Kino's find which holds his hopes for the future
17. _____ vs. Evil
18. Man vs. Society, for example
19. He finds the pearl
22. Kind of luck the pearl brings Kino's family
23. Place Kino is attacked and kills a man
24. Kino's house; symbol of good and tradition

The Pearl Crossword 3 Answer Key

		1 B	A	2 B	Y		3 E	D	U	C	4 A	T	5 I	O	N		
				U			V				R		M				
		6 C	O	Y	O	T	I	T	O		A		N				
		A		E			L				C		I				
		N		R			7 F				K		S		8 M		
		9 O	Y	10 S	T	E	R				E		C		A		
		E		O			11 S	C	O	R	P	I	O	N			
		12 F		M			H				S		E		13 P		
14 J	U	A	N	A							15 K	N	I	F	E		
				16 S	O	17 N	G	S		18 C		T			A		
		I				O		19 K		O					R		
20 G	U	L	F			O		I		21 N	O	V	E	L	L	A	
		Y		22 B	I	D		N		F							
				A		23 P	O	U	L	T	I	C	E				
		24 H	A	N	D			I									
		U				A		25 C	A	P	I	T	A	L			
		T				T		T									

Across
1. Coyotito; for example
3. Kino's dream for Coyotito
6. He is attacked by a scorpion
9. Natural home of the pearl
11. It attacked Coyotito
14. Kino's wife
15. Kino's weapon against the intruder
16. Music in the story
20. Final resting place of the pearl
21. Short novel
22. Competitive offer to purchase something
23. Seaweed pack on Coyotito's wound
24. Kino injures his on the doctor's gate
25. Place Kino hopes to sell the pearl

Down
2. They fix the market and cheat the villagers
3. Song of _____; a song of bad things
4. One kills Coyotito; Kino kills them
5. A point of view
6. Symbol of tradition; the old way of life
7. Symbolic of the natural way of the universe
8. I am the _____
10. Kino's brother; Juan ___
12. Song of the _____; a song of happiness and harmony
13. Kino's find which holds his hopes for the future
17. _____ vs. Evil
18. Man vs. Society; for example
19. He finds the pearl
22. Kind of luck the pearl brings Kino's family
23. Place Kino is attacked and kills a man
24. Kino's house; symbol of good and tradition

The Pearl Crossword 4

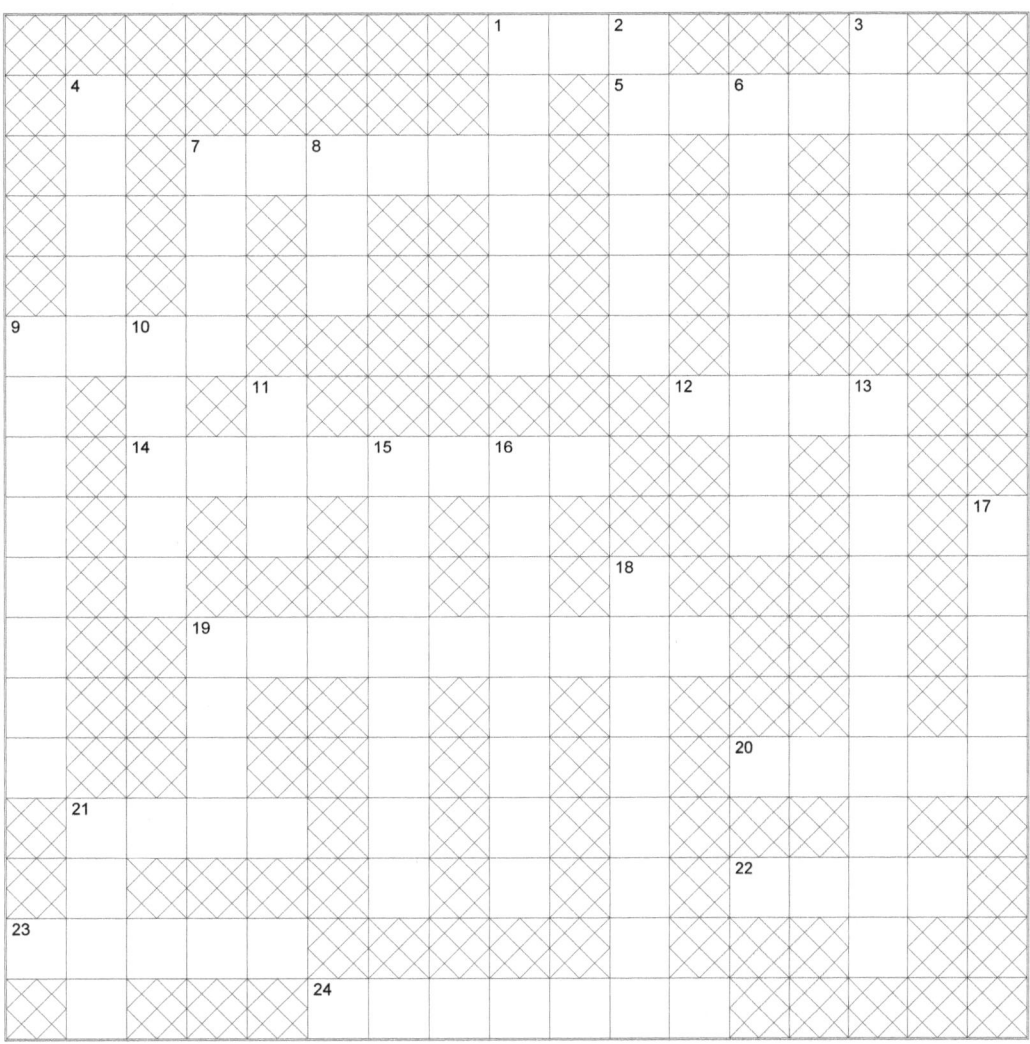

Across
1. Competitive offer to purchase something
5. Natural home of the pearl
7. Song of the _____; a song of happiness and harmony
9. Place Kino is attacked and kills a man
12. He finds the pearl
14. Place to which Kino, Juana and Coyotito flee
19. Kino's dream for Coyotito
20. Kino's weapon against the intruder
21. Final resting place of the pearl
22. Kino injures his on the doctor's gate
23. Music in the story
24. Fisherman's weapon Kino hopes to buy

Down
1. They fix the market and cheat the villagers
2. Refused to treat Coyotito at first
3. Kino's find which holds his hopes for the future
4. Kino's wife
6. It attacked Coyotito
7. Symbolic of the natural way of the universe
8. I am the _____
9. Seaweed pack on Coyotito's wound
10. Kino's brother; Juan ___
11. Kino's house; symbol of good and tradition
13. A point of view
15. One kills Coyotito; Kino kills them
16. Animal intuition
17. Symbol of tradition; the old way of life
18. He is attacked by a scorpion
19. Song of _____; a song of bad things
21. _____ vs. Evil

The Pearl Crossword 4 Answer Key

Across
1. Competitive offer to purchase something
5. Natural home of the pearl
7. Song of the _____; a song of happiness and harmony
9. Place Kino is attacked and kills a man
12. He finds the pearl
14. Place to which Kino, Juana and Coyotito flee
19. Kino's dream for Coyotito
20. Kino's weapon against the intruder
21. Final resting place of the pearl
22. Kino injures his ___ on the doctor's gate
23. Music in the story
24. Fisherman's weapon Kino hopes to buy

Down
1. They fix the market and cheat the villagers
2. Refused to treat Coyotito at first
3. Kino's find which holds his hopes for the future
4. Kino's wife
6. It attacked Coyotito
7. Symbolic of the natural way of the universe
8. I am the _____
9. Seaweed pack on Coyotito's wound
10. Kino's brother; Juan ___
11. Kino's house; symbol of good and tradition
13. A point of view
15. One kills Coyotito; Kino kills them
16. Animal intuition
17. Symbol of tradition, the old way of life
18. He is attacked by a scorpion
19. Song of _____; a song of bad things
21. _____ vs. Evil

Answers filled in grid:
- 1A. BID
- 5A. OYSTER
- 7A. FAMILY
- 9A. PATH
- 12A. KINO
- 14A. MOUNTAIN
- 19A. EDUCATION
- 20A. KNIFE
- 21A. GULF
- 22A. HAND
- 23A. SONGS
- 24A. HARPOON
- 1D. BUYERS
- 2D. DOCTORS
- 3D. PEARL
- 4D. JUANA
- 6D. SCORPION
- 7D. FISA(?)
- 8D. MANANTIAL
- 9D. POULTICE
- 10D. TOMAS
- 11D. HOUSE
- 13D. OPINION
- 15D. TRACKERS
- 16D. INSTINCT
- 17D. CANOE
- 18D. COYOTITO
- 19D. EVIL
- 21D. GOOD

44
Copyrighted

The Pearl

SONGS	KNIFE	CANOE	PATH	CONFLICT
HUT	INSTINCT	GOOD	HARPOON	POULTICE
TRACKERS	JUANA	FREE SPACE	FISH	TOWNSPEOPLE
BAD	SCORPION	PRIEST	DOCTOR	EVIL
CAPITAL	NOVELLA	MAN	TOMAS	BABY

The Pearl

GULF	BID	COYOTITO	MOUNTAIN	FAMILY
EDUCATION	BUYERS	PEARL	STEINBECK	KINO
HAND	OYSTER	FREE SPACE	TOMAS	MAN
NOVELLA	CAPITAL	EVIL	DOCTOR	PRIEST
SCORPION	BAD	TOWNSPEOPLE	FISH	OMNISCIENT

The Pearl

GULF	PATH	SCORPION	DOCTOR	OYSTER
CAPITAL	EVIL	EDUCATION	TOWNSPEOPLE	KINO
HAND	OMNISCIENT	FREE SPACE	CONFLICT	BID
MOUNTAIN	TOMAS	FAMILY	BABY	JUANA
KNIFE	TRACKERS	CANOE	POULTICE	HARPOON

The Pearl

SONGS	MAN	BUYERS	PEARL	NOVELLA
INSTINCT	GOOD	FISH	HUT	BAD
COYOTITO	PRIEST	FREE SPACE	POULTICE	CANOE
TRACKERS	KNIFE	JUANA	BABY	FAMILY
TOMAS	MOUNTAIN	BID	CONFLICT	STEINBECK

The Pearl

HARPOON	EVIL	TRACKERS	DOCTOR	GOOD
MAN	OMNISCIENT	GULF	PEARL	JUANA
EDUCATION	SCORPION	FREE SPACE	POULTICE	OYSTER
BAD	SONGS	CAPITAL	CONFLICT	COYOTITO
STEINBECK	NOVELLA	KINO	INSTINCT	CANOE

The Pearl

FISH	PRIEST	PATH	BABY	HUT
BID	TOMAS	TOWNSPEOPLE	KNIFE	HAND
MOUNTAIN	FAMILY	FREE SPACE	INSTINCT	KINO
NOVELLA	STEINBECK	COYOTITO	CONFLICT	CAPITAL
SONGS	BAD	OYSTER	POULTICE	BUYERS

The Pearl

DOCTOR	BUYERS	JUANA	KINO	BID
EDUCATION	HAND	OMNISCIENT	MOUNTAIN	GOOD
SONGS	PEARL	FREE SPACE	MAN	PRIEST
KNIFE	INSTINCT	FAMILY	CAPITAL	SCORPION
NOVELLA	TOWNSPEOPLE	TOMAS	PATH	FISH

The Pearl

STEINBECK	HUT	GULF	POULTICE	CANOE
TRACKERS	OYSTER	CONFLICT	COYOTITO	EVIL
HARPOON	BABY	FREE SPACE	PATH	TOMAS
TOWNSPEOPLE	NOVELLA	SCORPION	CAPITAL	FAMILY
INSTINCT	KNIFE	PRIEST	MAN	BAD

The Pearl

TOMAS	PEARL	CAPITAL	SONGS	TRACKERS
INSTINCT	EDUCATION	SCORPION	BABY	MAN
BAD	FISH	FREE SPACE	EVIL	MOUNTAIN
HARPOON	KNIFE	PATH	OYSTER	BUYERS
POULTICE	OMNISCIENT	DOCTOR	FAMILY	GULF

The Pearl

NOVELLA	HAND	STEINBECK	TOWNSPEOPLE	KINO
JUANA	COYOTITO	HUT	CONFLICT	CANOE
BID	PRIEST	FREE SPACE	FAMILY	DOCTOR
OMNISCIENT	POULTICE	BUYERS	OYSTER	PATH
KNIFE	HARPOON	MOUNTAIN	EVIL	GOOD

The Pearl

SCORPION	HARPOON	CONFLICT	SONGS	HUT
POULTICE	CANOE	GOOD	CAPITAL	MOUNTAIN
STEINBECK	NOVELLA	FREE SPACE	COYOTITO	BAD
FAMILY	EDUCATION	DOCTOR	GULF	BABY
TOWNSPEOPLE	BID	KINO	OMNISCIENT	MAN

The Pearl

HAND	OYSTER	INSTINCT	FISH	TOMAS
TRACKERS	PEARL	PRIEST	PATH	EVIL
KNIFE	JUANA	FREE SPACE	OMNISCIENT	KINO
BID	TOWNSPEOPLE	BABY	GULF	DOCTOR
EDUCATION	FAMILY	BAD	COYOTITO	BUYERS

The Pearl

INSTINCT	FAMILY	MAN	TRACKERS	BABY
HAND	JUANA	SCORPION	CANOE	KNIFE
GOOD	BUYERS	FREE SPACE	GULF	HARPOON
DOCTOR	EVIL	MOUNTAIN	COYOTITO	POULTICE
STEINBECK	OYSTER	PRIEST	NOVELLA	TOMAS

The Pearl

EDUCATION	TOWNSPEOPLE	FISH	HUT	CAPITAL
BAD	OMNISCIENT	KINO	CONFLICT	PATH
PEARL	BID	FREE SPACE	NOVELLA	PRIEST
OYSTER	STEINBECK	POULTICE	COYOTITO	MOUNTAIN
EVIL	DOCTOR	HARPOON	GULF	SONGS

The Pearl

CAPITAL	PATH	BUYERS	HARPOON	EVIL
FAMILY	POULTICE	CONFLICT	SCORPION	GULF
HAND	JUANA	FREE SPACE	PRIEST	TOWNSPEOPLE
KNIFE	DOCTOR	OMNISCIENT	MAN	FISH
EDUCATION	CANOE	BABY	HUT	OYSTER

The Pearl

BID	KINO	SONGS	STEINBECK	BAD
TOMAS	GOOD	TRACKERS	INSTINCT	PEARL
NOVELLA	COYOTITO	FREE SPACE	HUT	BABY
CANOE	EDUCATION	FISH	MAN	OMNISCIENT
DOCTOR	KNIFE	TOWNSPEOPLE	PRIEST	MOUNTAIN

The Pearl

JUANA	MOUNTAIN	BID	TOMAS	DOCTOR
MAN	CANOE	PRIEST	FAMILY	BUYERS
KINO	EDUCATION	FREE SPACE	PEARL	EVIL
FISH	KNIFE	GULF	OYSTER	SONGS
NOVELLA	HARPOON	HAND	TOWNSPEOPLE	BAD

The Pearl

CONFLICT	BABY	TRACKERS	PATH	SCORPION
POULTICE	COYOTITO	GOOD	HUT	OMNISCIENT
STEINBECK	INSTINCT	FREE SPACE	TOWNSPEOPLE	HAND
HARPOON	NOVELLA	SONGS	OYSTER	GULF
KNIFE	FISH	EVIL	PEARL	CAPITAL

The Pearl

DOCTOR	CANOE	CONFLICT	TOWNSPEOPLE	STEINBECK
GULF	TOMAS	CAPITAL	BAD	PEARL
KINO	MOUNTAIN	FREE SPACE	BABY	PATH
HAND	TRACKERS	OYSTER	HUT	SONGS
BID	KNIFE	FAMILY	PRIEST	HARPOON

The Pearl

FISH	JUANA	INSTINCT	EDUCATION	NOVELLA
GOOD	BUYERS	MAN	POULTICE	SCORPION
EVIL	OMNISCIENT	FREE SPACE	PRIEST	FAMILY
KNIFE	BID	SONGS	HUT	OYSTER
TRACKERS	HAND	PATH	BABY	COYOTITO

The Pearl

BAD	OYSTER	STEINBECK	OMNISCIENT	TOWNSPEOPLE
TOMAS	KINO	MOUNTAIN	FISH	PEARL
SONGS	MAN	FREE SPACE	KNIFE	POULTICE
BUYERS	GULF	FAMILY	EVIL	INSTINCT
HUT	CAPITAL	PRIEST	CONFLICT	BABY

The Pearl

BID	DOCTOR	JUANA	GOOD	TRACKERS
COYOTITO	SCORPION	HARPOON	CANOE	EDUCATION
PATH	NOVELLA	FREE SPACE	CONFLICT	PRIEST
CAPITAL	HUT	INSTINCT	EVIL	FAMILY
GULF	BUYERS	POULTICE	KNIFE	HAND

The Pearl

FAMILY	TOMAS	HARPOON	BAD	HAND
PEARL	KNIFE	PRIEST	CONFLICT	BABY
PATH	CANOE	FREE SPACE	INSTINCT	GOOD
OYSTER	POULTICE	KINO	NOVELLA	TOWNSPEOPLE
BID	FISH	STEINBECK	HUT	CAPITAL

The Pearl

OMNISCIENT	COYOTITO	TRACKERS	BUYERS	SONGS
MOUNTAIN	EDUCATION	JUANA	SCORPION	MAN
EVIL	DOCTOR	FREE SPACE	HUT	STEINBECK
FISH	BID	TOWNSPEOPLE	NOVELLA	KINO
POULTICE	OYSTER	GOOD	INSTINCT	GULF

The Pearl

FAMILY	CAPITAL	INSTINCT	GOOD	KINO
TRACKERS	BAD	NOVELLA	HARPOON	CANOE
POULTICE	MAN	FREE SPACE	DOCTOR	TOWNSPEOPLE
BUYERS	SCORPION	CONFLICT	OYSTER	JUANA
FISH	COYOTITO	SONGS	HUT	EDUCATION

The Pearl

EVIL	GULF	TOMAS	PATH	BABY
STEINBECK	KNIFE	OMNISCIENT	MOUNTAIN	PEARL
HAND	PRIEST	FREE SPACE	HUT	SONGS
COYOTITO	FISH	JUANA	OYSTER	CONFLICT
SCORPION	BUYERS	TOWNSPEOPLE	DOCTOR	BID

The Pearl

BAD	TRACKERS	INSTINCT	EVIL	CANOE
HUT	BUYERS	KNIFE	TOWNSPEOPLE	PATH
HAND	BABY	FREE SPACE	GOOD	OMNISCIENT
MAN	SONGS	CONFLICT	SCORPION	TOMAS
KINO	GULF	CAPITAL	PRIEST	FAMILY

The Pearl

PEARL	MOUNTAIN	COYOTITO	JUANA	STEINBECK
EDUCATION	BID	POULTICE	FISH	NOVELLA
HARPOON	DOCTOR	FREE SPACE	PRIEST	CAPITAL
GULF	KINO	TOMAS	SCORPION	CONFLICT
SONGS	MAN	OMNISCIENT	GOOD	OYSTER

The Pearl

OMNISCIENT	COYOTITO	PEARL	NOVELLA	HARPOON
CONFLICT	STEINBECK	JUANA	MAN	TOMAS
PRIEST	BAD	FREE SPACE	PATH	HAND
INSTINCT	MOUNTAIN	GULF	CAPITAL	HUT
BID	CANOE	POULTICE	EVIL	TOWNSPEOPLE

The Pearl

BUYERS	KINO	EDUCATION	SCORPION	FISH
FAMILY	GOOD	DOCTOR	BABY	OYSTER
TRACKERS	KNIFE	FREE SPACE	EVIL	POULTICE
CANOE	BID	HUT	CAPITAL	GULF
MOUNTAIN	INSTINCT	HAND	PATH	SONGS

The Pearl

EDUCATION	PRIEST	MAN	NOVELLA	FISH
HAND	SCORPION	MOUNTAIN	PATH	CAPITAL
DOCTOR	EVIL	FREE SPACE	JUANA	GOOD
OMNISCIENT	POULTICE	INSTINCT	BUYERS	COYOTITO
CANOE	HUT	HARPOON	FAMILY	TRACKERS

The Pearl

SONGS	PEARL	STEINBECK	BABY	TOWNSPEOPLE
TOMAS	KNIFE	GULF	BID	BAD
CONFLICT	OYSTER	FREE SPACE	FAMILY	HARPOON
HUT	CANOE	COYOTITO	BUYERS	INSTINCT
POULTICE	OMNISCIENT	GOOD	JUANA	KINO

The Pearl Vocabulary Word List

No.	Word	Clue/Definition
1.	ABANDONED	gave up; deserted
2.	APPREHENSIVELY	uneasily; fearfully
3.	AVARICE	too great a desire to have wealth and riches
4.	BROODING	thinking about same thing in a distressed way
5.	CEASELESS	unceasing; continual
6.	CLAMBERED	climbed with effort or clumsily
7.	COAGULATING	becoming a soft, semi-sold mass
8.	COMPARABLE	similar
9.	CONTEMPTUOUSLY	scornfully or disdainfully
10.	DISCONTENTEDLY	with dissatisfaction
11.	DISSEMBLING	concealing under a false appearance
12.	ESSENCE	the inward nature of anything
13.	EXHILARATION	a feeling of high spirits
14.	FRANTICALLY	wild with anger
15.	INCANDESCENCE	shining brilliantly
16.	UNDULATING	to cause to move in waves
17.	JUDICIOUS	wise and careful
18.	LAMENT	expression of deep sorrow by weeping or wailing
19.	LETHARGY	a condition of abnormal drowsiness
20.	LUCENT	shining; giving off light
21.	MERGED	joined together
22.	MONOLITHIC	made of a single block of stone
23.	MONOTONOUSLY	going in same tone without variation
24.	OBSCURED	covered over
25.	PERCEPTIBLE	able to be detected by the senses
26.	PERPLEXED	troubled with uncertainty
27.	PETULANT	impatient or irritable
28.	POULTICE	a hot moist mass of herbs
29.	PRECIPITATED	created
30.	PROPHECY	prediction
31.	REASSURING	restoring to confidence
32.	REMOTE	distant or secluded
33.	RESIDUE	that which is left after part is taken away
34.	RESINOUS	like resin, a semi-solid plant substance
35.	RUPTURE	crack; hole
36.	STRENUOUS	vigorous
37.	THRESHED	beat about; moved about violently
38.	TRANSFIGURED	changed in outward appearance
39.	WEARY	tired or worn out

The Pearl Vocabulary Fill In The Blank 1

_____ 1. troubled with uncertainty

_____ 2. wild with anger

_____ 3. a condition of abnormal drowsiness

_____ 4. restoring to confidence

_____ 5. to cause to move in waves

_____ 6. becoming a soft, semi-sold mass

_____ 7. tired or worn out

_____ 8. prediction

_____ 9. beat about; moved about violently

_____ 10. going in same tone without variation

_____ 11. vigorous

_____ 12. wise and careful

_____ 13. shining brilliantly

_____ 14. distant or secluded

_____ 15. covered over

_____ 16. crack; hole

_____ 17. thinking about same thing in a distressed way

_____ 18. able to be detected by the senses

_____ 19. concealing under a false appearance

_____ 20. climbed with effort or clumsily

The Pearl Vocabulary Fill In The Blank 1 Answer Key

PERPLEXED	1. troubled with uncertainty
FRANTICALLY	2. wild with anger
LETHARGY	3. a condition of abnormal drowsiness
REASSURING	4. restoring to confidence
UNDULATING	5. to cause to move in waves
COAGULATING	6. becoming a soft, semi-sold mass
WEARY	7. tired or worn out
PROPHECY	8. prediction
THRESHED	9. beat about; moved about violently
MONOTONOUSLY	10. going in same tone without variation
STRENUOUS	11. vigorous
JUDICIOUS	12. wise and careful
INCANDESCENCE	13. shining brilliantly
REMOTE	14. distant or secluded
OBSCURED	15. covered over
RUPTURE	16. crack; hole
BROODING	17. thinking about same thing in a distressed way
PERCEPTIBLE	18. able to be detected by the senses
DISSEMBLING	19. concealing under a false appearance
CLAMBERED	20. climbed with effort or clumsily

The Pearl Vocabulary Fill In The Blank 2

_____ 1. impatient or irritable

_____ 2. unceasing; continual

_____ 3. distant or secluded

_____ 4. joined together

_____ 5. shining brilliantly

_____ 6. the inward nature of anything

_____ 7. crack; hole

_____ 8. a feeling of high spirits

_____ 9. restoring to confidence

_____ 10. shining; giving off light

_____ 11. created

_____ 12. concealing under a false appearance

_____ 13. vigorous

_____ 14. troubled with uncertainty

_____ 15. thinking about same thing in a distressed way

_____ 16. to cause to move in waves

_____ 17. made of a single block of stone

_____ 18. tired or worn out

_____ 19. going in same tone without variation

_____ 20. beat about; moved about violently

The Pearl Vocabulary Fill In The Blank 2 Answer Key

PETULANT	1. impatient or irritable
CEASELESS	2. unceasing; continual
REMOTE	3. distant or secluded
MERGED	4. joined together
INCANDESCENCE	5. shining brilliantly
ESSENCE	6. the inward nature of anything
RUPTURE	7. crack; hole
EXHILARATION	8. a feeling of high spirits
REASSURING	9. restoring to confidence
LUCENT	10. shining; giving off light
PRECIPITATED	11. created
DISSEMBLING	12. concealing under a false appearance
STRENUOUS	13. vigorous
PERPLEXED	14. troubled with uncertainty
BROODING	15. thinking about same thing in a distressed way
UNDULATING	16. to cause to move in waves
MONOLITHIC	17. made of a single block of stone
WEARY	18. tired or worn out
MONOTONOUSLY	19. going in same tone without variation
THRESHED	20. beat about; moved about violently

The Pearl Vocabulary Fill In The Blank 3

1. the inward nature of anything
2. crack; hole
3. shining; giving off light
4. like resin, a semi-solid plant substance
5. to cause to move in waves
6. impatient or irritable
7. climbed with effort or clumsily
8. uneasily; fearfully
9. with dissatisfaction
10. that which is left after part is taken away
11. made of a single block of stone
12. too great a desire to have wealth and riches
13. vigorous
14. tired or worn out
15. going in same tone without variation
16. wise and careful
17. beat about; moved about violently
18. concealing under a false appearance
19. scornfully or disdainfully
20. troubled with uncertainty

The Pearl Vocabulary Fill In The Blank 3 Answer Key

ESSENCE	1. the inward nature of anything
RUPTURE	2. crack; hole
LUCENT	3. shining; giving off light
RESINOUS	4. like resin, a semi-solid plant substance
UNDULATING	5. to cause to move in waves
PETULANT	6. impatient or irritable
CLAMBERED	7. climbed with effort or clumsily
APPREHENSIVELY	8. uneasily; fearfully
DISCONTENTEDLY	9. with dissatisfaction
RESIDUE	10. that which is left after part is taken away
MONOLITHIC	11. made of a single block of stone
AVARICE	12. too great a desire to have wealth and riches
STRENUOUS	13. vigorous
WEARY	14. tired or worn out
MONOTONOUSLY	15. going in same tone without variation
JUDICIOUS	16. wise and careful
THRESHED	17. beat about; moved about violently
DISSEMBLING	18. concealing under a false appearance
CONTEMPTUOUSLY	19. scornfully or disdainfully
PERPLEXED	20. troubled with uncertainty

The Pearl Vocabulary Fill In The Blank 4

_____ 1. wise and careful

_____ 2. unceasing; continual

_____ 3. climbed with effort or clumsily

_____ 4. scornfully or disdainfully

_____ 5. distant or secluded

_____ 6. shining; giving off light

_____ 7. a feeling of high spirits

_____ 8. going in same tone without variation

_____ 9. a condition of abnormal drowsiness

_____ 10. vigorous

_____ 11. created

_____ 12. joined together

_____ 13. gave up; deserted

_____ 14. wild with anger

_____ 15. changed in outward appearance

_____ 16. troubled with uncertainty

_____ 17. a hot moist mass of herbs

_____ 18. covered over

_____ 19. with dissatisfaction

_____ 20. prediction

The Pearl Vocabulary Fill In The Blank 4 Answer Key

JUDICIOUS	1. wise and careful
CEASELESS	2. unceasing; continual
CLAMBERED	3. climbed with effort or clumsily
CONTEMPTUOUSLY	4. scornfully or disdainfully
REMOTE	5. distant or secluded
LUCENT	6. shining; giving off light
EXHILARATION	7. a feeling of high spirits
MONOTONOUSLY	8. going in same tone without variation
LETHARGY	9. a condition of abnormal drowsiness
STRENUOUS	10. vigorous
PRECIPITATED	11. created
MERGED	12. joined together
ABANDONED	13. gave up; deserted
FRANTICALLY	14. wild with anger
TRANSFIGURED	15. changed in outward appearance
PERPLEXED	16. troubled with uncertainty
POULTICE	17. a hot moist mass of herbs
OBSCURED	18. covered over
DISCONTENTEDLY	19. with dissatisfaction
PROPHECY	20. prediction

The Pearl Vocabulary Matching 1

___ 1. DISSEMBLING   A. thinking about same thing in a distressed way
___ 2. DISCONTENTEDLY   B. covered over
___ 3. RESINOUS   C. that which is left after part is taken away
___ 4. JUDICIOUS   D. with dissatisfaction
___ 5. COMPARABLE   E. created
___ 6. ESSENCE   F. changed in outward appearance
___ 7. OBSCURED   G. expression of deep sorrow by weeping or wailing
___ 8. EXHILARATION   H. uneasily; fearfully
___ 9. WEARY   I. the inward nature of anything
___10. APPREHENSIVELY   J. similar
___11. FRANTICALLY   K. a hot moist mass of herbs
___12. RUPTURE   L. crack; hole
___13. POULTICE   M. troubled with uncertainty
___14. LUCENT   N. impatient or irritable
___15. RESIDUE   O. prediction
___16. PRECIPITATED   P. concealing under a false appearance
___17. PERPLEXED   Q. a feeling of high spirits
___18. LAMENT   R. like resin, a semi-solid plant substance
___19. MERGED   S. shining brilliantly
___20. TRANSFIGURED   T. shining, giving off light
___21. INCANDESCENCE   U. gave up; deserted
___22. BROODING   V. wise and careful
___23. PETULANT   W. wild with anger
___24. PROPHECY   X. joined together
___25. ABANDONED   Y. tired or worn out

The Pearl Vocabulary Matching 1 Answer Key

P - 1.	DISSEMBLING	A. thinking about same thing in a distressed way
D - 2.	DISCONTENTEDLY	B. covered over
R - 3.	RESINOUS	C. that which is left after part is taken away
V - 4.	JUDICIOUS	D. with dissatisfaction
J - 5.	COMPARABLE	E. created
I - 6.	ESSENCE	F. changed in outward appearance
B - 7.	OBSCURED	G. expression of deep sorrow by weeping or wailing
Q - 8.	EXHILARATION	H. uneasily; fearfully
Y - 9.	WEARY	I. the inward nature of anything
H - 10.	APPREHENSIVELY	J. similar
W - 11.	FRANTICALLY	K. a hot moist mass of herbs
L - 12.	RUPTURE	L. crack; hole
K - 13.	POULTICE	M. troubled with uncertainty
T - 14.	LUCENT	N. impatient or irritable
C - 15.	RESIDUE	O. prediction
E - 16.	PRECIPITATED	P. concealing under a false appearance
M - 17.	PERPLEXED	Q. a feeling of high spirits
G - 18.	LAMENT	R. like resin, a semi-solid plant substance
X - 19.	MERGED	S. shining brilliantly
F - 20.	TRANSFIGURED	T. shining; giving off light
S - 21.	INCANDESCENCE	U. gave up; deserted
A - 22.	BROODING	V. wise and careful
N - 23.	PETULANT	W. wild with anger
O - 24.	PROPHECY	X. joined together
U - 25.	ABANDONED	Y. tired or worn out

The Pearl Vocabulary Matching 2

___ 1. UNDULATING   A. like resin, a semi-solid plant substance
___ 2. ESSENCE   B. crack; hole
___ 3. MERGED   C. made of a single block of stone
___ 4. RESIDUE   D. too great a desire to have wealth and riches
___ 5. RESINOUS   E. beat about; moved about violently
___ 6. COMPARABLE   F. created
___ 7. STRENUOUS   G. vigorous
___ 8. ABANDONED   H. shining; giving off light
___ 9. LAMENT   I. thinking about same thing in a distressed way
___ 10. THRESHED   J. impatient or irritable
___ 11. JUDICIOUS   K. that which is left after part is taken away
___ 12. REASSURING   L. similar
___ 13. DISSEMBLING   M. a feeling of high spirits
___ 14. PRECIPITATED   N. joined together
___ 15. BROODING   O. the inward nature of anything
___ 16. AVARICE   P. shining brilliantly
___ 17. PERPLEXED   Q. covered over
___ 18. LUCENT   R. to cause to move in waves
___ 19. INCANDESCENCE   S. expression of deep sorrow by weeping or wailing
___ 20. RUPTURE   T. troubled with uncertainty
___ 21. MONOLITHIC   U. concealing under a false appearance
___ 22. LETHARGY   V. restoring to confidence
___ 23. EXHILARATION   W. gave up; deserted
___ 24. PETULANT   X. a condition of abnormal drowsiness
___ 25. OBSCURED   Y. wise and careful

The Pearl Vocabulary Matching 2 Answer Key

R - 1. UNDULATING		A. like resin, a semi-solid plant substance
O - 2. ESSENCE		B. crack; hole
N - 3. MERGED		C. made of a single block of stone
K - 4. RESIDUE		D. too great a desire to have wealth and riches
A - 5. RESINOUS		E. beat about; moved about violently
L - 6. COMPARABLE		F. created
G - 7. STRENUOUS		G. vigorous
W - 8. ABANDONED		H. shining; giving off light
S - 9. LAMENT		I. thinking about same thing in a distressed way
E - 10. THRESHED		J. impatient or irritable
Y - 11. JUDICIOUS		K. that which is left after part is taken away
V - 12. REASSURING		L. similar
U - 13. DISSEMBLING		M. a feeling of high spirits
F - 14. PRECIPITATED		N. joined together
I - 15. BROODING		O. the inward nature of anything
D - 16. AVARICE		P. shining brilliantly
T - 17. PERPLEXED		Q. covered over
H - 18. LUCENT		R. to cause to move in waves
P - 19. INCANDESCENCE		S. expression of deep sorrow by weeping or wailing
B - 20. RUPTURE		T. troubled with uncertainty
C - 21. MONOLITHIC		U. concealing under a false appearance
X - 22. LETHARGY		V. restoring to confidence
M - 23. EXHILARATION		W. gave up; deserted
J - 24. PETULANT		X. a condition of abnormal drowsiness
Q - 25. OBSCURED		Y. wise and careful

The Pearl Vocabulary Matching 3

___ 1. INCANDESCENCE   A. similar
___ 2. ABANDONED   B. crack; hole
___ 3. CLAMBERED   C. changed in outward appearance
___ 4. JUDICIOUS   D. created
___ 5. OBSCURED   E. joined together
___ 6. THRESHED   F. expression of deep sorrow by weeping or wailing
___ 7. UNDULATING   G. climbed with effort or clumsily
___ 8. RESIDUE   H. tired or worn out
___ 9. APPREHENSIVELY   I. wise and careful
___10. CEASELESS   J. covered over
___11. RUPTURE   K. troubled with uncertainty
___12. LAMENT   L. beat about; moved about violently
___13. WEARY   M. prediction
___14. COAGULATING   N. gave up; deserted
___15. PETULANT   O. restoring to confidence
___16. EXHILARATION   P. to cause to move in waves
___17. COMPARABLE   Q. unceasing; continual
___18. PROPHECY   R. that which is left after part is taken away
___19. TRANSFIGURED   S. uneasily; fearfully
___20. PERPLEXED   T. able to be detected by the senses
___21. PERCEPTIBLE   U. becoming a soft, semi-sold mass
___22. MERGED   V. a feeling of high spirits
___23. REASSURING   W. with dissatisfaction
___24. DISCONTENTEDLY   X. shining brilliantly
___25. PRECIPITATED   Y. impatient or irritable

The Pearl Vocabulary Matching 3 Answer Key

X - 1. INCANDESCENCE		A. similar
N - 2. ABANDONED		B. crack; hole
G - 3. CLAMBERED		C. changed in outward appearance
I - 4. JUDICIOUS		D. created
J - 5. OBSCURED		E. joined together
L - 6. THRESHED		F. expression of deep sorrow by weeping or wailing
P - 7. UNDULATING		G. climbed with effort or clumsily
R - 8. RESIDUE		H. tired or worn out
S - 9. APPREHENSIVELY		I. wise and careful
Q - 10. CEASELESS		J. covered over
B - 11. RUPTURE		K. troubled with uncertainty
F - 12. LAMENT		L. beat about; moved about violently
H - 13. WEARY		M. prediction
U - 14. COAGULATING		N. gave up; deserted
Y - 15. PETULANT		O. restoring to confidence
V - 16. EXHILARATION		P. to cause to move in waves
A - 17. COMPARABLE		Q. unceasing; continual
M - 18. PROPHECY		R. that which is left after part is taken away
C - 19. TRANSFIGURED		S. uneasily; fearfully
K - 20. PERPLEXED		T. able to be detected by the senses
T - 21. PERCEPTIBLE		U. becoming a soft, semi-sold mass
E - 22. MERGED		V. a feeling of high spirits
O - 23. REASSURING		W. with dissatisfaction
W - 24. DISCONTENTEDLY		X. shining brilliantly
D - 25. PRECIPITATED		Y. impatient or irritable

The Pearl Vocabulary Matching 4

___ 1. PRECIPITATED   A. made of a single block of stone
___ 2. STRENUOUS   B. a hot moist mass of herbs
___ 3. OBSCURED   C. covered over
___ 4. BROODING   D. to cause to move in waves
___ 5. DISSEMBLING   E. changed in outward appearance
___ 6. CLAMBERED   F. beat about; moved about violently
___ 7. THRESHED   G. scornfully or disdainfully
___ 8. AVARICE   H. distant or secluded
___ 9. RUPTURE   I. thinking about same thing in a distressed way
___10. FRANTICALLY   J. vigorous
___11. APPREHENSIVELY   K. concealing under a false appearance
___12. MERGED   L. uneasily; fearfully
___13. CONTEMPTUOUSLY   M. crack; hole
___14. UNDULATING   N. climbed with effort or clumsily
___15. LAMENT   O. unceasing; continual
___16. ESSENCE   P. wild with anger
___17. PERPLEXED   Q. joined together
___18. PROPHECY   R. going in same tone without variation
___19. ABANDONED   S. prediction
___20. POULTICE   T. the inward nature of anything
___21. REMOTE   U. troubled with uncertainty
___22. TRANSFIGURED   V. expression of deep sorrow by weeping or wailing
___23. MONOTONOUSLY   W. too great a desire to have wealth and riches
___24. CEASELESS   X. gave up; deserted
___25. MONOLITHIC   Y. created

The Pearl Vocabulary Matching 4 Answer Key

Y - 1.	PRECIPITATED	A. made of a single block of stone
J - 2.	STRENUOUS	B. a hot moist mass of herbs
C - 3.	OBSCURED	C. covered over
I - 4.	BROODING	D. to cause to move in waves
K - 5.	DISSEMBLING	E. changed in outward appearance
N - 6.	CLAMBERED	F. beat about; moved about violently
F - 7.	THRESHED	G. scornfully or disdainfully
W - 8.	AVARICE	H. distant or secluded
M - 9.	RUPTURE	I. thinking about same thing in a distressed way
P - 10.	FRANTICALLY	J. vigorous
L - 11.	APPREHENSIVELY	K. concealing under a false appearance
Q - 12.	MERGED	L. uneasily; fearfully
G - 13.	CONTEMPTUOUSLY	M. crack; hole
D - 14.	UNDULATING	N. climbed with effort or clumsily
V - 15.	LAMENT	O. unceasing; continual
T - 16.	ESSENCE	P. wild with anger
U - 17.	PERPLEXED	Q. joined together
S - 18.	PROPHECY	R. going in same tone without variation
X - 19.	ABANDONED	S. prediction
B - 20.	POULTICE	T. the inward nature of anything
H - 21.	REMOTE	U. troubled with uncertainty
E - 22.	TRANSFIGURED	V. expression of deep sorrow by weeping or wailing
R - 23.	MONOTONOUSLY	W. too great a desire to have wealth and riches
O - 24.	CEASELESS	X. gave up; deserted
A - 25.	MONOLITHIC	Y. created

The Pearl Vocabulary Magic Squares 1

Match the definition with the vocabulary word. Put your answers in the magic squares below. When your answers are correct, all columns and rows will add to the same number.

A. LETHARGY
B. WEARY
C. CONTEMPTUOUSLY
D. JUDICIOUS
E. LUCENT
F. RESINOUS
G. PRECIPITATED
H. INCANDESCENCE
I. APPREHENSIVELY
J. REMOTE
K. CLAMBERED
L. MONOTONOUSLY
M. THRESHED
N. PERPLEXED
O. ABANDONED
P. PERCEPTIBLE

1. like resin, a semi-solid plant substance
2. uneasily; fearfully
3. gave up; deserted
4. wise and careful
5. beat about; moved about violently
6. tired or worn out
7. shining brilliantly
8. climbed with effort or clumsily
9. scornfully or disdainfully
10. able to be detected by the senses
11. distant or secluded
12. shining; giving off light
13. going in same tone without variation
14. created
15. a condition of abnormal drowsiness
16. troubled with uncertainty

A=	B=	C=	D=
E=	F=	G=	H=
I=	J=	K=	L=
M=	N=	O=	P=

The Pearl Vocabulary Magic Squares 1 Answer Key

Match the definition with the vocabulary word. Put your answers in the magic squares below. When your answers are correct, all columns and rows will add to the same number.

A. LETHARGY
B. WEARY
C. CONTEMPTUOUSLY
D. JUDICIOUS
E. LUCENT
F. RESINOUS
G. PRECIPITATED
H. INCANDESCENCE
I. APPREHENSIVELY
J. REMOTE
K. CLAMBERED
L. MONOTONOUSLY
M. THRESHED
N. PERPLEXED
O. ABANDONED
P. PERCEPTIBLE

1. like resin, a semi-solid plant substance
2. uneasily; fearfully
3. gave up; deserted
4. wise and careful
5. beat about; moved about violently
6. tired or worn out
7. shining brilliantly
8. climbed with effort or clumsily
9. scornfully or disdainfully
10. able to be detected by the senses
11. distant or secluded
12. shining; giving off light
13. going in same tone without variation
14. created
15. a condition of abnormal drowsiness
16. troubled with uncertainty

A=15	B=6	C=9	D=4
E=12	F=1	G=14	H=7
I=2	J=11	K=8	L=13
M=5	N=16	O=3	P=10

The Pearl Vocabulary Magic Squares 2

Match the definition with the vocabulary word. Put your answers in the magic squares below. When your answers are correct, all columns and rows will add to the same number.

A. LUCENT
B. BROODING
C. OBSCURED
D. ABANDONED
E. ESSENCE
F. CONTEMPTUOUSLY
G. LETHARGY
H. STRENUOUS
I. THRESHED
J. PROPHECY
K. JUDICIOUS
L. COAGULATING
M. UNDULATING
N. LAMENT
O. PERCEPTIBLE
P. RUPTURE

1. vigorous
2. to cause to move in waves
3. thinking about same thing in a distressed way
4. wise and careful
5. prediction
6. covered over
7. crack; hole
8. the inward nature of anything
9. able to be detected by the senses
10. scornfully or disdainfully
11. beat about; moved about violently
12. gave up; deserted
13. shining; giving off light
14. becoming a soft, semi-sold mass
15. a condition of abnormal drowsiness
16. expression of deep sorrow by weeping or wailing

A=	B=	C=	D=
E=	F=	G=	H=
I=	J=	K=	L=
M=	N=	O=	P=

The Pearl Vocabulary Magic Squares 2 Answer Key

Match the definition with the vocabulary word. Put your answers in the magic squares below. When your answers are correct, all columns and rows will add to the same number.

A. LUCENT
B. BROODING
C. OBSCURED
D. ABANDONED
E. ESSENCE
F. CONTEMPTUOUSLY
G. LETHARGY
H. STRENUOUS
I. THRESHED
J. PROPHECY
K. JUDICIOUS
L. COAGULATING
M. UNDULATING
N. LAMENT
O. PERCEPTIBLE
P. RUPTURE

1. vigorous
2. to cause to move in waves
3. thinking about same thing in a distressed way
4. wise and careful
5. prediction
6. covered over
7. crack; hole
8. the inward nature of anything
9. able to be detected by the senses
10. scornfully or disdainfully
11. beat about; moved about violently
12. gave up; deserted
13. shining; giving off light
14. becoming a soft, semi-sold mass
15. a condition of abnormal drowsiness
16. expression of deep sorrow by weeping or wailing

A=13	B=3	C=6	D=12
E=8	F=10	G=15	H=1
I=11	J=5	K=4	L=14
M=2	N=16	O=9	P=7

The Pearl Vocabulary Magic Squares 3

Match the definition with the vocabulary word. Put your answers in the magic squares below. When your answers are correct, all columns and rows will add to the same number.

A. FRANTICALLY
B. LETHARGY
C. STRENUOUS
D. REASSURING
E. WEARY
F. DISCONTENTEDLY
G. OBSCURED
H. CLAMBERED
I. COMPARABLE
J. MONOLITHIC
K. LAMENT
L. MERGED
M. THRESHED
N. PETULANT
O. PRECIPITATED
P. RUPTURE

1. wild with anger
2. impatient or irritable
3. made of a single block of stone
4. tired or worn out
5. covered over
6. joined together
7. crack; hole
8. vigorous
9. created
10. restoring to confidence
11. climbed with effort or clumsily
12. expression of deep sorrow by weeping or wailing
13. similar
14. with dissatisfaction
15. a condition of abnormal drowsiness
16. beat about; moved about violently

A=	B=	C=	D=
E=	F=	G=	H=
I=	J=	K=	L=
M=	N=	O=	P=

The Pearl Vocabulary Magic Squares 3 Answer Key

Match the definition with the vocabulary word. Put your answers in the magic squares below. When your answers are correct, all columns and rows will add to the same number.

A. FRANTICALLY
B. LETHARGY
C. STRENUOUS
D. REASSURING
E. WEARY
F. DISCONTENTEDLY
G. OBSCURED
H. CLAMBERED
I. COMPARABLE
J. MONOLITHIC
K. LAMENT
L. MERGED
M. THRESHED
N. PETULANT
O. PRECIPITATED
P. RUPTURE

1. wild with anger
2. impatient or irritable
3. made of a single block of stone
4. tired or worn out
5. covered over
6. joined together
7. crack; hole
8. vigorous
9. created
10. restoring to confidence
11. climbed with effort or clumsily
12. expression of deep sorrow by weeping or wailing
13. similar
14. with dissatisfaction
15. a condition of abnormal drowsiness
16. beat about; moved about violently

A=1	B=15	C=8	D=10
E=4	F=14	G=5	H=11
I=13	J=3	K=12	L=6
M=16	N=2	O=9	P=7

The Pearl Vocabulary Magic Squares 4

Match the definition with the vocabulary word. Put your answers in the magic squares below. When your answers are correct, all columns and rows will add to the same number.

A. APPREHENSIVELY
B. CEASELESS
C. INCANDESCENCE
D. WEARY
E. ESSENCE
F. MONOTONOUSLY

G. DISCONTENTEDLY
H. PERCEPTIBLE
I. RESINOUS
J. COAGULATING
K. POULTICE
L. ABANDONED

M. MERGED
N. DISSEMBLING
O. PETULANT
P. FRANTICALLY

1. impatient or irritable
2. tired or worn out
3. becoming a soft, semi-sold mass
4. the inward nature of anything
5. like resin, a semi-solid plant substance
6. going in same tone without variation
7. wild with anger
8. shining brilliantly
9. able to be detected by the senses
10. a hot moist mass of herbs
11. uneasily; fearfully
12. concealing under a false appearance
13. unceasing; continual
14. joined together
15. with dissatisfaction
16. gave up; deserted

A=	B=	C=	D=
E=	F=	G=	H=
I=	J=	K=	L=
M=	N=	O=	P=

The Pearl Vocabulary Magic Squares 4 Answer Key

Match the definition with the vocabulary word. Put your answers in the magic squares below. When your answers are correct, all columns and rows will add to the same number.

A. APPREHENSIVELY
B. CEASELESS
C. INCANDESCENCE
D. WEARY
E. ESSENCE
F. MONOTONOUSLY
G. DISCONTENTEDLY
H. PERCEPTIBLE
I. RESINOUS
J. COAGULATING
K. POULTICE
L. ABANDONED
M. MERGED
N. DISSEMBLING
O. PETULANT
P. FRANTICALLY

1. impatient or irritable
2. tired or worn out
3. becoming a soft, semi-sold mass
4. the inward nature of anything
5. like resin, a semi-solid plant substance
6. going in same tone without variation
7. wild with anger
8. shining brilliantly
9. able to be detected by the senses
10. a hot moist mass of herbs
11. uneasily; fearfully
12. concealing under a false appearance
13. unceasing; continual
14. joined together
15. with dissatisfaction
16. gave up; deserted

A=11	B=13	C=8	D=2
E=4	F=6	G=15	H=9
I=5	J=3	K=10	L=16
M=14	N=12	O=1	P=7

The Pearl Vocabulary Word Search 1

Words are placed backwards, forward, diagonally, up and down. Clues listed below can help you find the words. Circle the hidden vocabulary words in the maze.

```
S T R E N U O U S E X H I L A R A T I O N
R Y G G C P C P R E C I P I T A T E D Z B
W V B F J L E A P P R E H E N S I V E L Y
W W J G R F Y S J F R Q O T L J T C S G H
C Z G Z K R P P S C M P Y B Q L K L D X R
W M W N S A V R E E Y C K P S S U X D U Z
J W Z X G N M P R U N R W A E C T C P N B
F J F D P T T P E D M C D V N T U T E C V
J U D I C I O U S I O R E A S S U R I N G
B N E C B C D S I S N E N R F R N L E L T
P M R L J A E G N E O M O I E D D P A D X
X N E Q Q L Y N O R L O D C D I U O C N Y
C Y B J E L K I U L I T N E Z S L U O M T
K T M S Y Y V D S E T E A H C S A L M E C
T T A H T L S O Y T H C B M D E T T P R X
Q E L G W B Q O R H I N A W T M I I A G C
C Y C E H P O R P A C H E N S B N C R E C
P X D M R Y S B X R Y A E Z W L G E A D X
M T W S G X D H F G R M C B X I N M B V W
P E R P L E X E D Y A B Y N X N D J L M S
T H R E S H E D D L T D G K S G T K E C K
```

a condition of abnormal drowsiness (8)
a feeling of high spirits (12)
a hot moist mass of herbs (8)
able to be detected by the senses (11)
beat about; moved about violently (8)
climbed with effort or clumsily (9)
concealing under a false appearance (11)
covered over (8)
crack; hole (7)
created (12)
distant or secluded (6)
expression of deep sorrow by weeping or wailing (6)
gave up; deserted (9)
impatient or irritable (8)
joined together (6)
like resin, a semi-solid plant substance (8)
made of a single block of stone (10)
prediction (8)

restoring to confidence (10)
shining; giving off light (6)
similar (10)
that which is left after part is taken away (7)
the inward nature of anything (7)
thinking about same thing in a distressed way (8)
tired or worn out (5)
to cause to move in waves (10)
too great a desire to have wealth and riches (7)
troubled with uncertainty (9)
unceasing; continual (9)
uneasily; fearfully (14)
vigorous (9)
wild with anger (11)
wise and careful (9)

The Pearl Vocabulary Word Search 1 Answer Key

Words are placed backwards, forward, diagonally, up and down. Clues listed below can help you find the words. Circle the hidden vocabulary words in the maze.

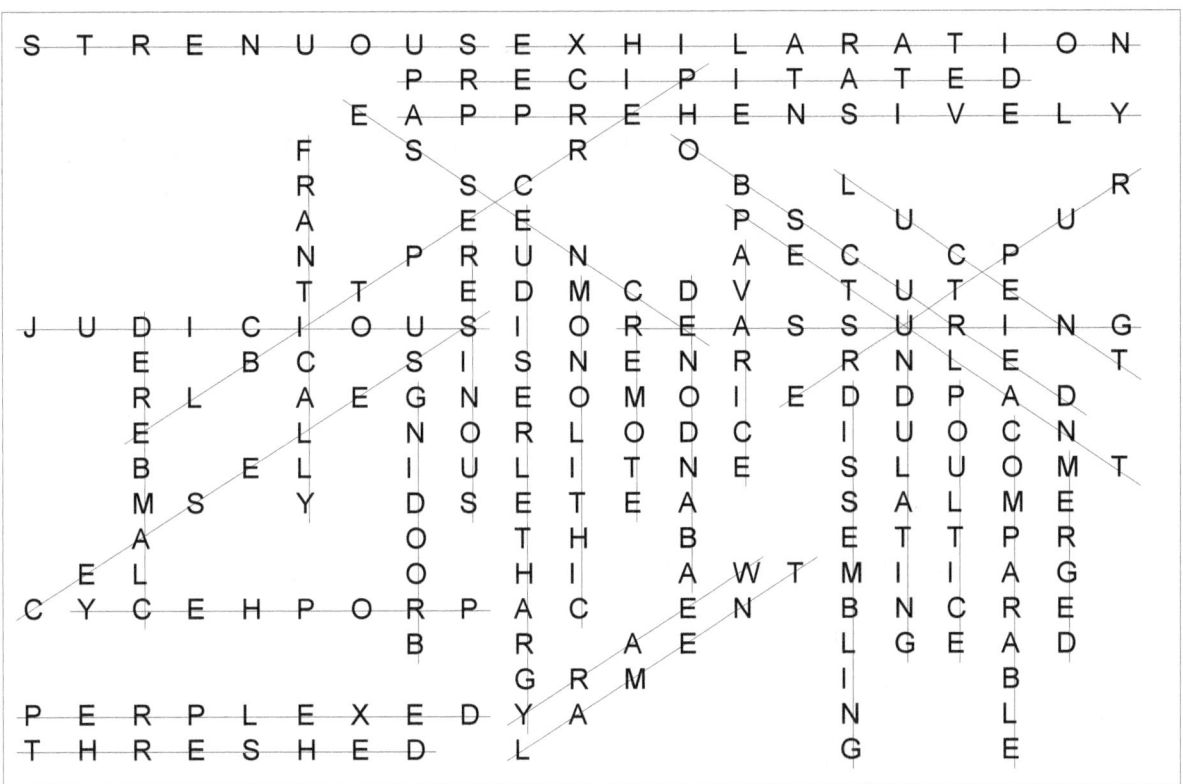

a condition of abnormal drowsiness (8)
a feeling of high spirits (12)
a hot moist mass of herbs (8)
able to be detected by the senses (11)
beat about; moved about violently (8)
climbed with effort or clumsily (9)
concealing under a false appearance (11)
covered over (8)
crack; hole (7)
created (12)
distant or secluded (6)
expression of deep sorrow by weeping or wailing (6)
gave up; deserted (9)
impatient or irritable (8)
joined together (6)
like resin, a semi-solid plant substance (8)
made of a single block of stone (10)
prediction (8)

restoring to confidence (10)
shining; giving off light (6)
similar (10)
that which is left after part is taken away (7)
the inward nature of anything (7)
thinking about same thing in a distressed way (8)
tired or worn out (5)
to cause to move in waves (10)
too great a desire to have wealth and riches (7)
troubled with uncertainty (9)
unceasing; continual (9)
uneasily; fearfully (14)
vigorous (9)
wild with anger (11)
wise and careful (9)

The Pearl Vocabulary Word Search 2

Words are placed backwards, forward, diagonally, up and down. Clues listed below can help you find the words. Circle the hidden vocabulary words in the maze.

```
P D P R E C I P I T A T E D D T P Y L D L
J V E S X Y F N C C S O H E N J E L M G V
Q W R Q H G G D O B S B H P M U R S B W Y
S H C J I F X M Q R Q S E K C D P U D C R
Y M E S L N P K Z F E C I H T I L O N O M
G Z P C A A C R Z R N U D V W C E U L Q C
R Z T X R H N K H E E R P M Y I X T Y L G
A Y I A A D F T C W C E Z C G O E P A R L
H M B P T M S Y G I D A N W U D M E U G
T L L I R E G M Q T W I V E S B E S P Y
E R E R O D A T N J L R Z H A E H T S T C
L U C E N T T N A L U T E P R R S N E U O
X Z C A A Q J E S S O N F E Y U I O N R A
G J C E B T C M S F P Q D T O L F C C E G
N N C Z A C W A E F I E S U O N I S E R U
I Z R H N S E L Q R U G N G L D G T X L L
D H T D D R E M V D G E U J R A O T S S A
O L C F O Q J L I N R E M R Y M T K N F T
O W C X N C H S E T K W D N E W Z I G Y I
R G K G E Q E X S S H R M R X D P H N P N
B C H X D R X C H G S P R O P H E C Y G G
```

a condition of abnormal drowsiness (8)
a feeling of high spirits (12)
a hot moist mass of herbs (8)
able to be detected by the senses (11)
beat about; moved about violently (8)
becoming a soft, semi-sold mass (11)
changed in outward appearance (12)
climbed with effort or clumsily (9)
covered over (8)
crack; hole (7)
created (12)
distant or secluded (6)
expression of deep sorrow by weeping or wailing (6)
gave up; deserted (9)
impatient or irritable (8)
joined together (6)
like resin, a semi-solid plant substance (8)
made of a single block of stone (10)

prediction (8)
restoring to confidence (10)
scornfully or disdainfully (14)
shining brilliantly (13)
shining; giving off light (6)
similar (10)
that which is left after part is taken away (7)
the inward nature of anything (7)
thinking about same thing in a distressed way (8)
tired or worn out (5)
to cause to move in waves (10)
too great a desire to have wealth and riches (7)
troubled with uncertainty (9)
unceasing; continual (9)
vigorous (9)
wise and careful (9)

The Pearl Vocabulary Word Search 2 Answer Key

Words are placed backwards, forward, diagonally, up and down. Clues listed below can help you find the words. Circle the hidden vocabulary words in the maze.

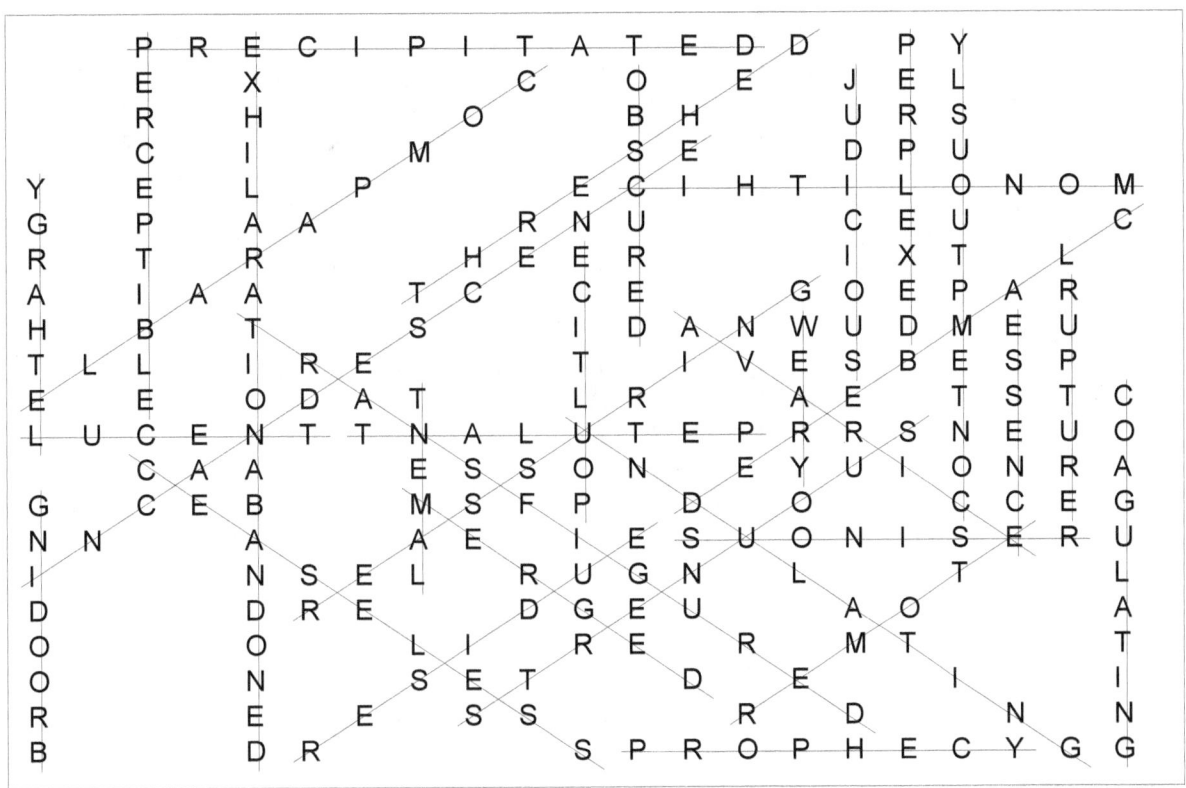

a condition of abnormal drowsiness (8)
a feeling of high spirits (12)
a hot moist mass of herbs (8)
able to be detected by the senses (11)
beat about; moved about violently (8)
becoming a soft, semi-sold mass (11)
changed in outward appearance (12)
climbed with effort or clumsily (9)
covered over (8)
crack; hole (7)
created (12)
distant or secluded (6)
expression of deep sorrow by weeping or wailing (6)
gave up; deserted (9)
impatient or irritable (8)
joined together (6)
like resin, a semi-solid plant substance (8)
made of a single block of stone (10)

prediction (8)
restoring to confidence (10)
scornfully or disdainfully (14)
shining brilliantly (13)
shining; giving off light (6)
similar (10)
that which is left after part is taken away (7)
the inward nature of anything (7)
thinking about same thing in a distressed way (8)
tired or worn out (5)
to cause to move in waves (10)
too great a desire to have wealth and riches (7)
troubled with uncertainty (9)
unceasing; continual (9)
vigorous (9)
wise and careful (9)

The Pearl Vocabulary Word Search 3

Words are placed backwards, forward, diagonally, up and down. Words listed below are included in the maze. Circle the hidden vocabulary words in the maze.

```
P O U L T I C E X H I L A R A T I O N Z A H
F E S S E N C E V E L B A R A P M O C Z P F
H F J T Z S Y L S U O U T P M E T N O C P S
Y L S U O N O T O N O M G Q Y R B O N M R Z
J R V M D K T T M C Z N B G F P P B B P E T
R E L R L I Q W C X I J R P N L W S L E H M
J A B J Y V C C B L M A F L T E K C A R E S
B S F J G G T I B Q H T Z R Q X B U M C N J
R S Z G S D W M O T F R A L C E C R E E S P
O U M D M G E H E U G N S T N D T E N P I M
O R C E A S E L E S S T R V H M Y D T T V R
D I Z R S K W X F F K G P E G R E F P I E Z
I N R I D V F Y I L A E C N M R E R D B L S
N G D K C L H G Q S T B I W E O Y S G L Y P
G N I T A L U D N U T T A B E C T Y H E N H
C X R H P R K C L S A R M N Q A C E J E D L
D K U B E T J A E L Z A E F D E R L M C D S
V Y P D T D N W U N L S B N H O J Y G I S L
F K T G N T C G S C T Y F P U N N W D R M D
W Y U Y P H A N G G V S O K Z O X E D A R Q
R R R S U O N I S E R R E S I D U E D V T D
W N E W C P R E C I P I T A T E D S F A S R
```

ABANDONED	JUDICIOUS	PROPHECY
APPREHENSIVELY	LAMENT	REASSURING
AVARICE	LETHARGY	REMOTE
BROODING	LUCENT	RESIDUE
CEASELESS	MERGED	RESINOUS
CLAMBERED	MONOTONOUSLY	RUPTURE
COAGULATING	OBSCURED	STRENUOUS
COMPARABLE	PERCEPTIBLE	THRESHED
CONTEMPTUOUSLY	PERPLEXED	TRANSFIGURED
DISSEMBLING	PETULANT	UNDULATING
ESSENCE	POULTICE	WEARY
EXHILARATION	PRECIPITATED	

The Pearl Vocabulary Word Search 3 Answer Key

Words are placed backwards, forward, diagonally, up and down. Words listed below are included in the maze. Circle the hidden vocabulary words in the maze.

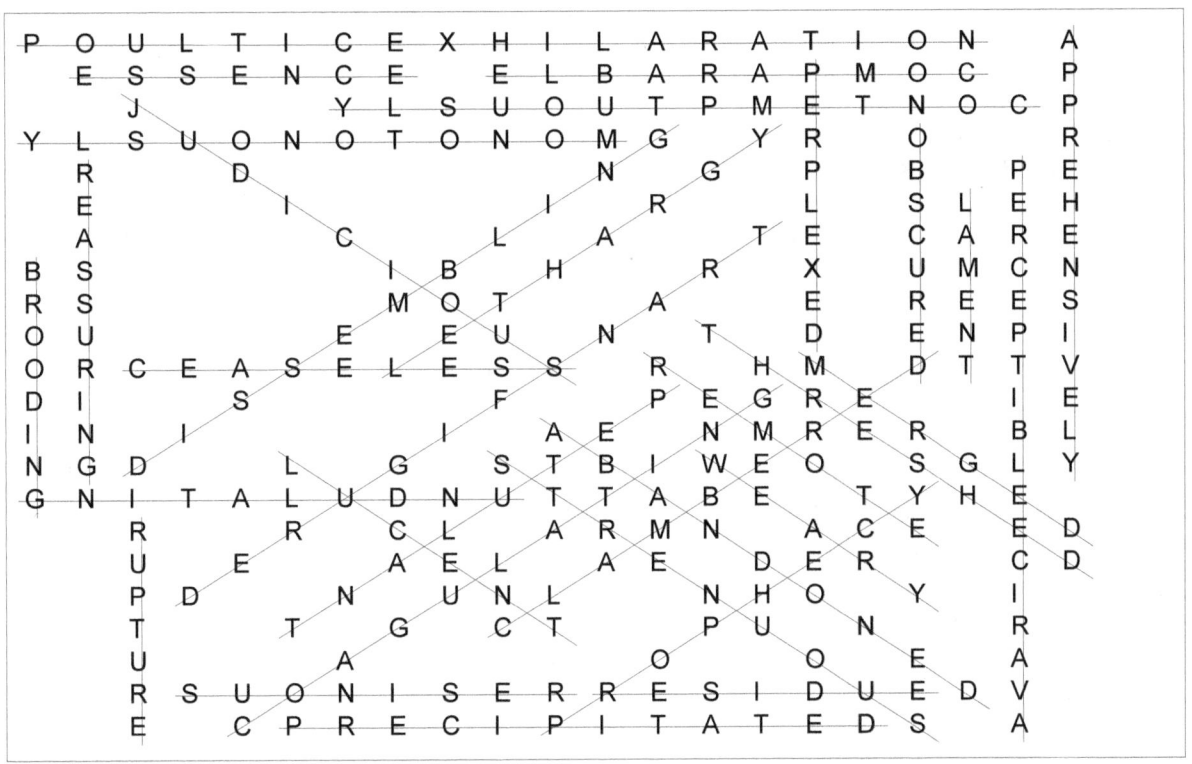

ABANDONED	JUDICIOUS	PROPHECY
APPREHENSIVELY	LAMENT	REASSURING
AVARICE	LETHARGY	REMOTE
BROODING	LUCENT	RESIDUE
CEASELESS	MERGED	RESINOUS
CLAMBERED	MONOTONOUSLY	RUPTURE
COAGULATING	OBSCURED	STRENUOUS
COMPARABLE	PERCEPTIBLE	THRESHED
CONTEMPTUOUSLY	PERPLEXED	TRANSFIGURED
DISSEMBLING	PETULANT	UNDULATING
ESSENCE	POULTICE	WEARY
EXHILARATION	PRECIPITATED	

The Pearl Vocabulary Word Search 4

Words are placed backwards, forward, diagonally, up and down. Words listed below are included in the maze. Circle the hidden vocabulary words in the maze.

```
P R O P H E C Y X S U P E T U L A N T D B V
V L C X P L Y L D E T N E T N O C S I D T L
G T L Y F L G G S F F F D R B V V G S T C R
F R A N T I C A L L Y P L U C M W R Q K J K
C O M P A R A B L E R C P J L E Q T M Y X R
G P B G N I L B M E S S I D K A P T P L G E
C P E G B X X W C V Y T R M V P T T D R F S
V O R M T K K I J X S R X R Z D D I I S X I
L U E J C H P W C C N E P K L Y F S N B L D
M L D C T I R P S D W N T Q S D U Y Z G L U
G T V X T P F E E G Y U B R O O D I N G J E
B I H A Y J V G S V R O V R I Z B J M N C X
R C T S R P R D W H A U S C S M L J X I L H
P E R P L E X E D R E S I N O U S V R T E W
D R M W M B A E N Z W D R N C S L A N A T T
D U H O Z Q N S E L U Q O E E H V E G L H Q
F T T N T O P C S J B L N L F A M C L U A K
H P J L D E N C X U I T E T W A L R B G R J
D U D N B E X K M T R S P K L T Q S T A G D
T R A B S B Q G H P A I D E R U C S B O Y C
H B W S F R H I L E W Y N P J T S C D C S R
A X E B W N C N C D E R U G I F S N A R T Z
```

ABANDONED	LAMENT	REASSURING
AVARICE	LETHARGY	REMOTE
BROODING	LUCENT	RESIDUE
CEASELESS	MERGED	RESINOUS
CLAMBERED	MONOLITHIC	RUPTURE
COAGULATING	OBSCURED	STRENUOUS
COMPARABLE	PERCEPTIBLE	THRESHED
DISCONTENTEDLY	PERPLEXED	TRANSFIGURED
DISSEMBLING	PETULANT	UNDULATING
ESSENCE	POULTICE	WEARY
FRANTICALLY	PRECIPITATED	
JUDICIOUS	PROPHECY	

The Pearl Vocabulary Word Search 4 Answer Key

Words are placed backwards, forward, diagonally, up and down. Words listed below are included in the maze. Circle the hidden vocabulary words in the maze.

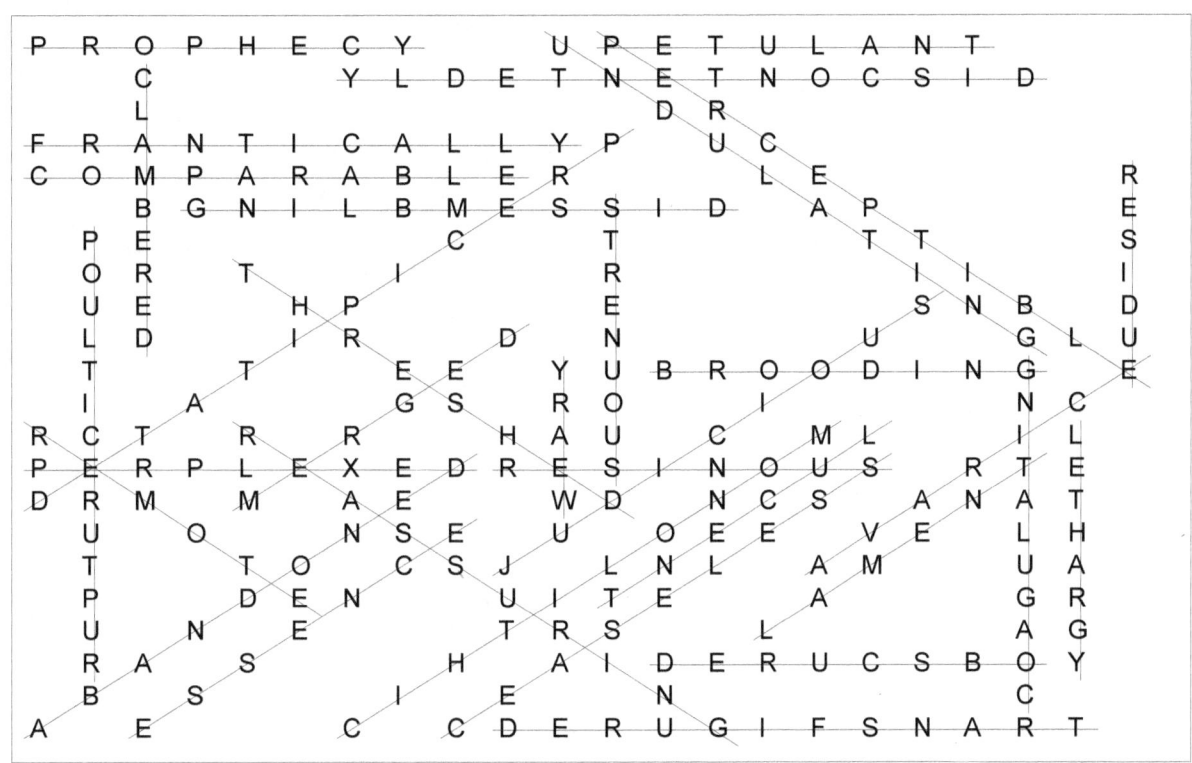

ABANDONED	LAMENT	REASSURING
AVARICE	LETHARGY	REMOTE
BROODING	LUCENT	RESIDUE
CEASELESS	MERGED	RESINOUS
CLAMBERED	MONOLITHIC	RUPTURE
COAGULATING	OBSCURED	STRENUOUS
COMPARABLE	PERCEPTIBLE	THRESHED
DISCONTENTEDLY	PERPLEXED	TRANSFIGURED
DISSEMBLING	PETULANT	UNDULATING
ESSENCE	POULTICE	WEARY
FRANTICALLY	PRECIPITATED	
JUDICIOUS	PROPHECY	

The Pearl Vocabulary Crossword 1

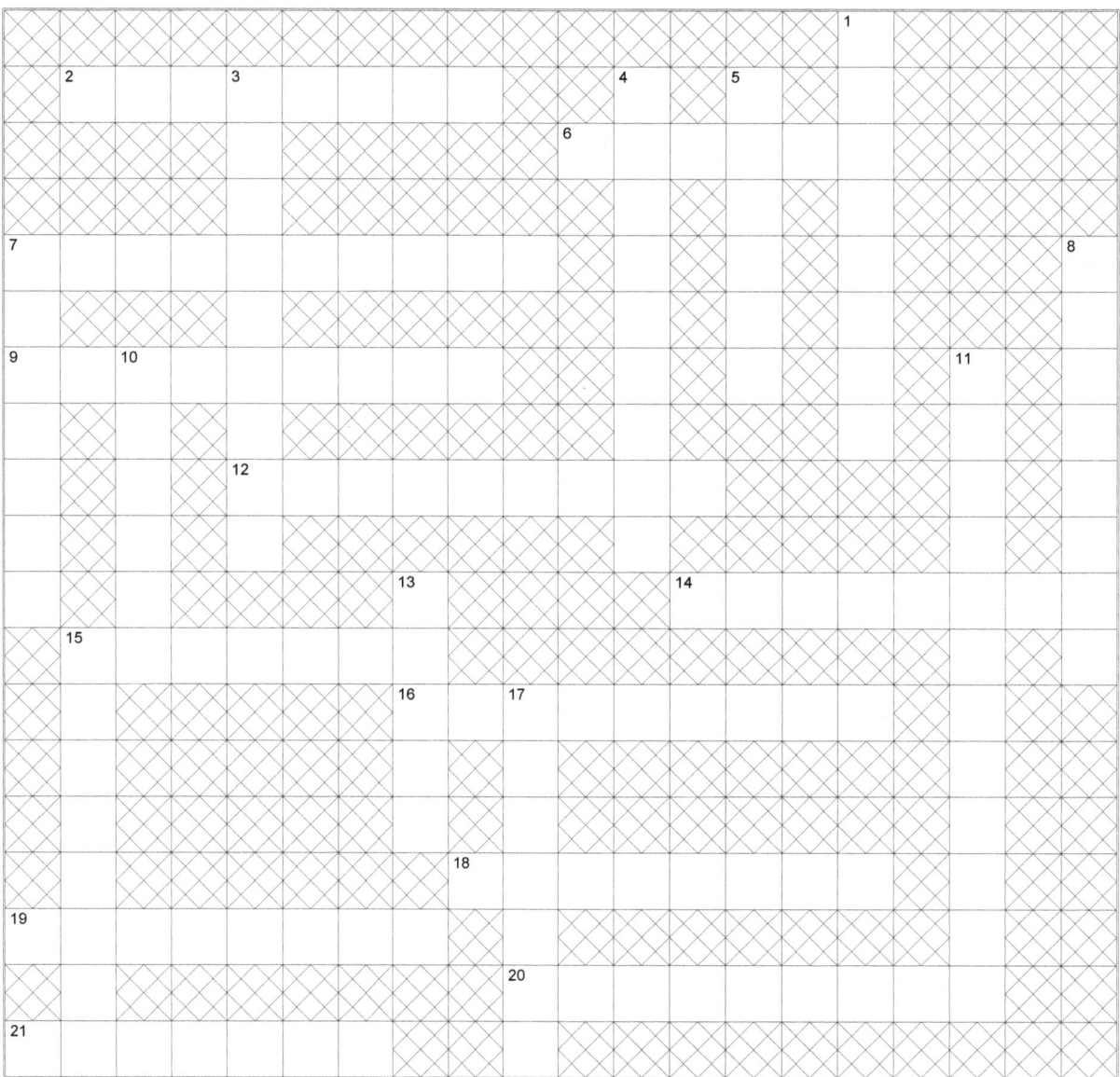

Across
2. covered over
6. shining; giving off light
7. restoring to confidence
9. troubled with uncertainty
12. vigorous
14. thinking about same thing in a distressed way
15. that which is left after part is taken away
16. gave up; deserted
18. prediction
19. a hot moist mass of herbs
20. climbed with effort or clumsily
21. the inward nature of anything

Down
1. impatient or irritable
3. unceasing; continual
4. wise and careful
5. joined together
7. crack; hole
8. a condition of abnormal drowsiness
10. distant or secluded
11. created
13. tired or worn out
15. like resin, a semi-solid plant substance
17. too great a desire to have wealth and riches

The Pearl Vocabulary Crossword 1 Answer Key

														P	
	O	B	S	C	U	R	E	D		J		M		E	
			E						L	U	C	E	N	T	
			A						D		R		U		
R	E	A	S	S	U	R	I	N	G	I		G		L		L
U			E						C		E		A			E
P	E	R	P	L	E	X	E	D		I		D		N	P		T
T		E		E						O				T	R		H
U		M		S	T	R	E	N	U	O	U	S			E		A
R		O		S						S					C		R
E		T						W				B	R	O	O	D	I	N	G
	R	E	S	I	D	U	E								P		Y
	E						A	B	A	N	D	O	N	E	D	I	
	S						R		V						T	
	I						Y		A						A	
	N							P	R	O	P	H	E	C	Y	T	
P	O	U	L	T	I	C	E		I						E	
	U								C	L	A	M	B	E	R	E	D
E	S	S	E	N	C	E		E								

Across
2. covered over
6. shining; giving off light
7. restoring to confidence
9. troubled with uncertainty
12. vigorous
14. thinking about same thing in a distressed way
15. that which is left after part is taken away
16. gave up; deserted
18. prediction
19. a hot moist mass of herbs
20. climbed with effort or clumsily
21. the inward nature of anything

Down
1. impatient or irritable
3. unceasing; continual
4. wise and careful
5. joined together
7. crack; hole
8. a condition of abnormal drowsiness
10. distant or secluded
11. created
13. tired or worn out
15. like resin, a semi-solid plant substance
17. too great a desire to have wealth and riches

The Pearl Vocabulary Crossword 2

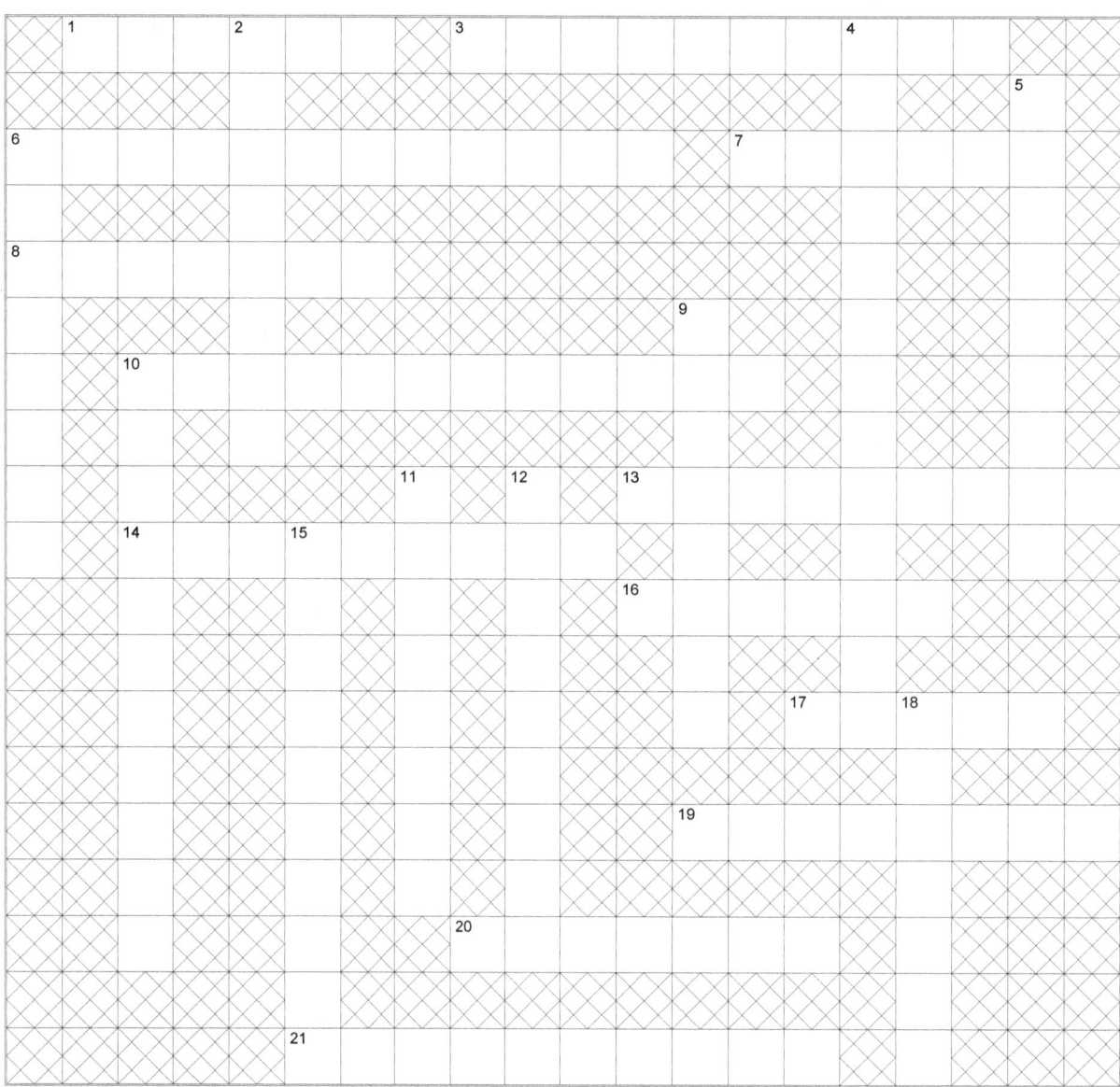

Across
1. distant or secluded
3. to cause to move in waves
6. changed in outward appearance
7. shining; giving off light
8. crack; hole
10. created
13. wise and careful
14. climbed with effort or clumsily
16. expression of deep sorrow by weeping or wailing
17. tired or worn out
19. a condition of abnormal drowsiness
20. the inward nature of anything
21. similar

Down
2. covered over
4. shining brilliantly
5. vigorous
6. beat about; moved about violently
9. impatient or irritable
10. able to be detected by the senses
11. like resin, a semi-solid plant substance
12. unceasing; continual
15. made of a single block of stone
18. too great a desire to have wealth and riches

The Pearl Vocabulary Crossword 2 Answer Key

Across
1. distant or secluded
3. to cause to move in waves
6. changed in outward appearance
7. shining; giving off light
8. crack; hole
10. created
13. wise and careful
14. climbed with effort or clumsily
16. expression of deep sorrow by weeping or wailing
17. tired or worn out
19. a condition of abnormal drowsiness
20. the inward nature of anything
21. similar

Down
2. covered over
4. shining brilliantly
5. vigorous
6. beat about; moved about violently
9. impatient or irritable
10. able to be detected by the senses
11. like resin, a semi-solid plant substance
12. unceasing; continual
15. made of a single block of stone
18. too great a desire to have wealth and riches

The Pearl Vocabulary Crossword 3

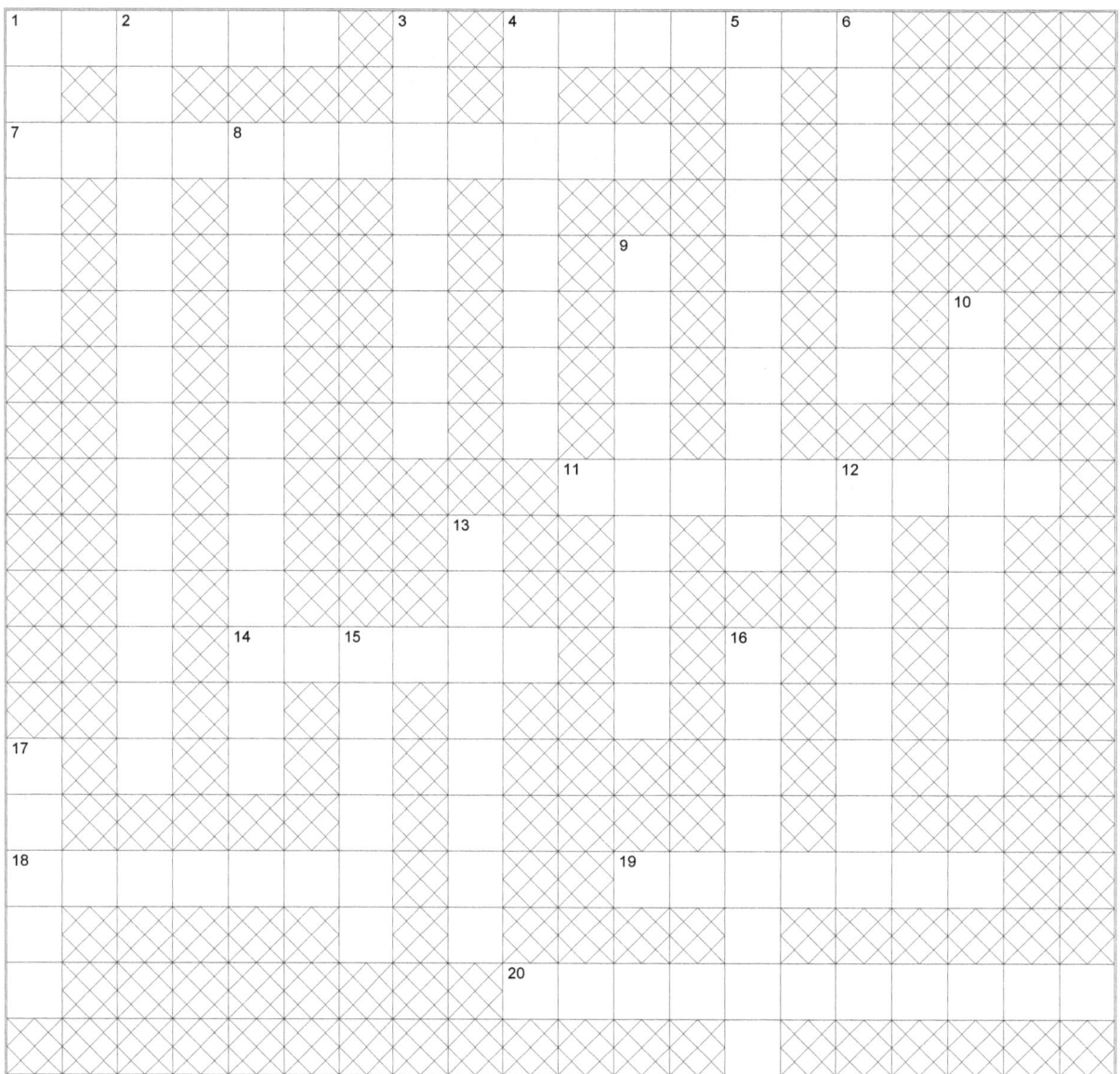

Across
1. shining; giving off light
4. crack; hole
7. going in same tone without variation
11. gave up, deserted
14. distant or secluded
18. too great a desire to have wealth and riches
19. that which is left after part is taken away
20. concealing under a false appearance

Down
1. expression of deep sorrow by weeping or wailing
2. scornfully or disdainfully
3. thinking about same thing in a distressed way
4. like resin, a semi-solid plant substance
5. to cause to move in waves
6. the inward nature of anything
8. changed in outward appearance
9. climbed with effort or clumsily
10. vigorous
12. covered over
13. a condition of abnormal drowsiness
15. joined together
16. beat about; moved about violently
17. tired or worn out

The Pearl Vocabulary Crossword 3 Answer Key

Across
1. shining, giving off light
4. crack; hole
7. going in same tone without variation
11. gave up; deserted
14. distant or secluded
18. too great a desire to have wealth and riches
19. that which is left after part is taken away
20. concealing under a false appearance

Down
1. expression of deep sorrow by weeping or wailing
2. scornfully or disdainfully
3. thinking about same thing in a distressed way
4. like resin, a semi-solid plant substance
5. to cause to move in waves
6. the inward nature of anything
8. changed in outward appearance
9. climbed with effort or clumsily
10. vigorous
12. covered over
13. a condition of abnormal drowsiness
15. joined together
16. beat about; moved about violently
17. tired or worn out

The Pearl Vocabulary Crossword 4

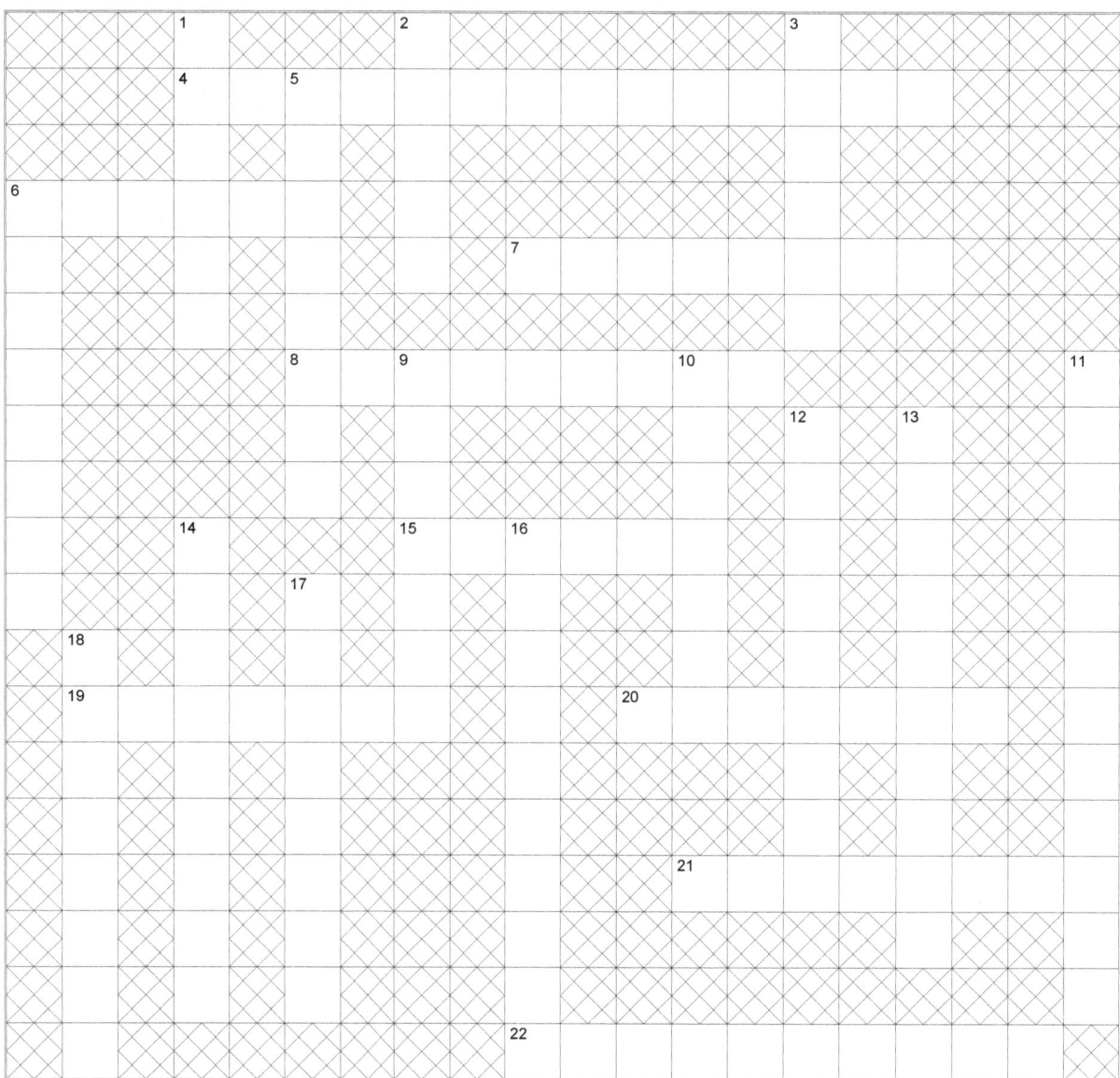

Across
4. uneasily; fearfully
6. shining; giving off light
7. prediction
8. gave up; deserted
15. distant or secluded
19. crack; hole
20. that which is left after part is taken away
21. like resin, a semi-solid plant substance
22. similar

Down
1. expression of deep sorrow by weeping or wailing
2. tired or worn out
3. joined together
5. impatient or irritable
6. a condition of abnormal drowsiness
9. too great a desire to have wealth and riches
10. the inward nature of anything
11. going in same tone without variation
12. wise and careful
13. restoring to confidence
14. troubled with uncertainty
16. made of a single block of stone
17. a hot moist mass of herbs
18. thinking about same thing in a distressed way

The Pearl Vocabulary Crossword 4 Answer Key

Across
4. uneasily; fearfully
6. shining; giving off light
7. prediction
8. gave up; deserted
15. distant or secluded
19. crack; hole
20. that which is left after part is taken away
21. like resin, a semi-solid plant substance
22. similar

Down
1. expression of deep sorrow by weeping or wailing
2. tired or worn out
3. joined together
5. impatient or irritable
6. a condition of abnormal drowsiness
9. too great a desire to have wealth and riches
10. the inward nature of anything
11. going in same tone without variation
12. wise and careful
13. restoring to confidence
14. troubled with uncertainty
16. made of a single block of stone
17. a hot moist mass of herbs
18. thinking about same thing in a distressed way

The Pearl Vocabulary Juggle Letters 1

1. SBREODCU = 1. _____
covered over

2. ARYWE = 2. _____
tired or worn out

3. LSNDEMSIIGB = 3. _____
concealing under a false appearance

4. ERUSNISO = 4. _____
like resin, a semi-solid plant substance

5. UIJSDOICU = 5. _____
wise and careful

6. XEDPRLEEP = 6. _____
troubled with uncertainty

7. MAAOBLECRP = 7. _____
similar

8. PCEEPIRBLTE = 8. _____
able to be detected by the senses

9. ESNESEC = 9. _____
the inward nature of anything

10. DEMEGR = 10. _____
joined together

11. ECRLDAMBE = 11. _____
climbed with effort or clumsily

12. ETEOMR = 12. _____
distant or secluded

13. CITTNODEYLENSD = 13. _____
with dissatisfaction

14. IMTOHLIOCN = 14. _____
made of a single block of stone

15. HENIOAXITALR = 15. _____
a feeling of high spirits

The Pearl Vocabulary Juggle Letters 1 Answer Key

1. SBREODCU = 1. OBSCURED
   covered over

2. ARYWE = 2. WEARY
   tired or worn out

3. LSNDEMSIIGB = 3. DISSEMBLING
   concealing under a false appearance

4. ERUSNISO = 4. RESINOUS
   like resin, a semi-solid plant substance

5. UIJSDOICU = 5. JUDICIOUS
   wise and careful

6. XEDPRLEEP = 6. PERPLEXED
   troubled with uncertainty

7. MAAOBLECRP = 7. COMPARABLE
   similar

8. PCEEPIRBLTE = 8. PERCEPTIBLE
   able to be detected by the senses

9. ESNESEC = 9. ESSENCE
   the inward nature of anything

10. DEMEGR = 10. MERGED
    joined together

11. ECRLDAMBE = 11. CLAMBERED
    climbed with effort or clumsily

12. ETEOMR = 12. REMOTE
    distant or secluded

13. CITTNODEYLENSD = 13. DISCONTENTEDLY
    with dissatisfaction

14. IMTOHLIOCN = 14. MONOLITHIC
    made of a single block of stone

15. HENIOAXITALR = 15. EXHILARATION
    a feeling of high spirits

The Pearl Vocabulary Juggle Letters 2

1. ELESSASEC = 1. _____
   unceasing; continual

2. YEPCPOHR = 2. _____
   prediction

3. PDLEXREEP = 3. _____
   troubled with uncertainty

4. EHTEHDRS = 4. _____
   beat about; moved about violently

5. SENUISRO = 5. _____
   like resin, a semi-solid plant substance

6. EREOMT = 6. _____
   distant or secluded

7. UOBERSDC = 7. _____
   covered over

8. ONYOUOTMSOLN = 8. _____
   going in same tone without variation

9. ALMNET = 9. _____
   expression of deep sorrow by weeping or wailing

10. EUTLPATN = 10. _____
    impatient or irritable

11. HELGYTRA = 11. _____
    a condition of abnormal drowsiness

12. EIEARVELHNPSPY = 12. _____
    uneasily; fearfully

13. LAERBDMEC = 13. _____
    climbed with effort or clumsily

14. TRUURPE = 14. _____
    crack; hole

15. IBSLNSEDIMG = 15. _____
    concealing under a false appearance

The Pearl Vocabulary Juggle Letters 2 Answer Key

1. ELESSASEC = 1. CEASELESS
   unceasing; continual

2. YEPCPOHR = 2. PROPHECY
   prediction

3. PDLEXREEP = 3. PERPLEXED
   troubled with uncertainty

4. EHTEHDRS = 4. THRESHED
   beat about; moved about violently

5. SENUISRO = 5. RESINOUS
   like resin, a semi-solid plant substance

6. EREOMT = 6. REMOTE
   distant or secluded

7. UOBERSDC = 7. OBSCURED
   covered over

8. ONYOUOTMSOLN = 8. MONOTONOUSLY
   going in same tone without variation

9. ALMNET = 9. LAMENT
   expression of deep sorrow by weeping or wailing

10. EUTLPATN = 10. PETULANT
    impatient or irritable

11. HELGYTRA = 11. LETHARGY
    a condition of abnormal drowsiness

12. EIEARVELHNPSPY = 12. APPREHENSIVELY
    uneasily; fearfully

13. LAERBDMEC = 13. CLAMBERED
    climbed with effort or clumsily

14. TRUURPE = 14. RUPTURE
    crack; hole

15. IBSLNSEDIMG = 15. DISSEMBLING
    concealing under a false appearance

The Pearl Vocabulary Juggle Letters 3

1. NLTAUTEP = 1. _____
   impatient or irritable

2. COUBRSDE = 2. _____
   covered over

3. DOENNAADB = 3. _____
   gave up; deserted

4. BEILRTEEPPC = 4. _____
   able to be detected by the senses

5. ICDENSEACNCNE = 5. _____
   shining brilliantly

6. GISNSDLMBIE = 6. _____
   concealing under a false appearance

7. OOMTCSPULUYETN = 7. _____
   scornfully or disdainfully

8. EELRXDPEP = 8. _____
   troubled with uncertainty

9. RIDOBOGN = 9. _____
   thinking about same thing in a distressed way

10. IRCVAEA = 10. _____
    too great a desire to have wealth and riches

11. IEALSYPPNEREHV = 11. _____
    uneasily; fearfully

12. CTMOONHILI = 12. _____
    made of a single block of stone

13. EEMDGR = 13. _____
    joined together

14. AGIUUNLDNT = 14. _____
    to cause to move in waves

15. UNGRFDSERAIT = 15. _____
    changed in outward appearance

The Pearl Vocabulary Juggle Letters 3 Answer Key

1. NLTAUTEP = 1. PETULANT
   impatient or irritable

2. COUBRSDE = 2. OBSCURED
   covered over

3. DOENNAADB = 3. ABANDONED
   gave up; deserted

4. BEILRTEEPPC = 4. PERCEPTIBLE
   able to be detected by the senses

5. ICDENSEACNCNE = 5. INCANDESCENCE
   shining brilliantly

6. GISNSDLMBIE = 6. DISSEMBLING
   concealing under a false appearance

7. OOMTCSPULUYETN = 7. CONTEMPTUOUSLY
   scornfully or disdainfully

8. EELRXDPEP = 8. PERPLEXED
   troubled with uncertainty

9. RIDOBOGN = 9. BROODING
   thinking about same thing in a distressed way

10. IRCVAEA = 10. AVARICE
    too great a desire to have wealth and riches

11. IEALSYPPNEREHV = 11. APPREHENSIVELY
    uneasily; fearfully

12. CTMOONHILI = 12. MONOLITHIC
    made of a single block of stone

13. EEMDGR = 13. MERGED
    joined together

14. AGIUUNLDNT = 14. UNDULATING
    to cause to move in waves

15. UNGRFDSERAIT = 15. TRANSFIGURED
    changed in outward appearance

The Pearl Vocabulary Juggle Letters 4

1. PLHPAEYRISVEEN = 1. _____
   uneasily; fearfully

2. RWEAY = 2. _____
   tired or worn out

3. RPOPHECY = 3. _____
   prediction

4. UEROSDCB = 4. _____
   covered over

5. AEENINSENDCCC = 5. _____
   shining brilliantly

6. LMACARBPEO = 6. _____
   similar

7. ETEIRLBCPEP = 7. _____
   able to be detected by the senses

8. ENIYEOTDLTSDNC = 8. _____
   with dissatisfaction

9. SECNEES = 9. _____
   the inward nature of anything

10. IEDESRU = 10. _____
    that which is left after part is taken away

11. AIIOHRTALEXN = 11. _____
    a feeling of high spirits

12. RPTIPEIADCET = 12. _____
    created

13. DIBNOROG = 13. _____
    thinking about same thing in a distressed way

14. IICHLOMNOT = 14. _____
    made of a single block of stone

15. ERDGME = 15. _____
    joined together

The Pearl Vocabulary Juggle Letters 4 Answer Key

1. PLHPAEYRISVEEN = 1. APPREHENSIVELY
   uneasily; fearfully

2. RWEAY = 2. WEARY
   tired or worn out

3. RPOPHECY = 3. PROPHECY
   prediction

4. UEROSDCB = 4. OBSCURED
   covered over

5. AEENINSENDCCC = 5. INCANDESCENCE
   shining brilliantly

6. LMACARBPEO = 6. COMPARABLE
   similar

7. ETEIRLBCPEP = 7. PERCEPTIBLE
   able to be detected by the senses

8. ENIYEOTDLTSDNC = 8. DISCONTENTEDLY
   with dissatisfaction

9. SECNEES = 9. ESSENCE
   the inward nature of anything

10. IEDESRU = 10. RESIDUE
    that which is left after part is taken away

11. AIIOHRTALEXN = 11. EXHILARATION
    a feeling of high spirits

12. RPTIPEIADCET = 12. PRECIPITATED
    created

13. DIBNOROG = 13. BROODING
    thinking about same thing in a distressed way

14. IICHLOMNOT = 14. MONOLITHIC
    made of a single block of stone

15. ERDGME = 15. MERGED
    joined together

ABANDONED	gave up; deserted
APPREHENSIVELY	uneasily; fearfully
AVARICE	too great a desire to have wealth and riches
BROODING	thinking about same thing in a distressed way
CEASELESS	unceasing; continual
CLAMBERED	climbed with effort or clumsily
COAGULATING	becoming a soft, semi-sold mass

COMPARABLE	similar
CONTEMPTUOUSLY	scornfully or disdainfully
DISCONTENTEDLY	with dissatisfaction
DISSEMBLING	concealing under a false appearance
ESSENCE	the inward nature of anything
EXHILARATION	a feeling of high spirits
FRANTICALLY	wild with anger

INCANDESCENCE	shining brilliantly
JUDICIOUS	wise and careful
LAMENT	expression of deep sorrow by weeping or wailing
LETHARGY	a condition of abnormal drowsiness
LUCENT	shining; giving off light
MERGED	joined together
MONOLITHIC	made of a single block of stone

MONOTONOUSLY	going in same tone without variation
OBSCURED	covered over
PERCEPTIBLE	able to be detected by the senses
PERPLEXED	troubled with uncertainty
PETULANT	impatient or irritable
POULTICE	a hot moist mass of herbs
PRECIPITATED	created

PROPHECY	prediction
REASSURING	restoring to confidence
REMOTE	distant or secluded
RESIDUE	that which is left after part is taken away
RESINOUS	like resin, a semi-solid plant substance
RUPTURE	crack; hole
STRENUOUS	vigorous

THRESHED	beat about; moved about violently
TRANSFIGURED	changed in outward appearance
UNDULATING	to cause to move in waves
WEARY	tired or worn out

The Pearl Vocabulary

MONOLITHIC	INCANDESCENCE	PERPLEXED	CLAMBERED	POULTICE
FRANTICALLY	PRECIPITATED	RUPTURE	LAMENT	OBSCURED
LUCENT	UNDULATING	FREE SPACE	AVARICE	JUDICIOUS
MONOTONOUSLY	ABANDONED	REMOTE	DISCONTENTEDLY	STRENUOUS
WEARY	APPREHENSIVELY	BROODING	PROPHECY	ESSENCE

The Pearl Vocabulary

PERCEPTIBLE	COMPARABLE	LETHARGY	MERGED	DISSEMBLING
REASSURING	EXHILARATION	RESIDUE	TRANSFIGURED	CONTEMPTUOUSLY
THRESHED	RESINOUS	FREE SPACE	CEASELESS	ESSENCE
PROPHECY	BROODING	APPREHENSIVELY	WEARY	STRENUOUS
DISCONTENTEDLY	REMOTE	ABANDONED	MONOTONOUSLY	JUDICIOUS

The Pearl Vocabulary

FRANTICALLY	ABANDONED	DISCONTENTEDLY	RESINOUS	EXHILARATION
LUCENT	RESIDUE	LETHARGY	TRANSFIGURED	POULTICE
CLAMBERED	CONTEMPTUOUSLY	FREE SPACE	PERCEPTIBLE	MONOLITHIC
PERPLEXED	RUPTURE	DISSEMBLING	REMOTE	APPREHENSIVELY
STRENUOUS	THRESHED	ESSENCE	PETULANT	WEARY

The Pearl Vocabulary

COMPARABLE	PROPHECY	LAMENT	OBSCURED	PRECIPITATED
UNDULATING	MERGED	JUDICIOUS	BROODING	MONOTONOUSLY
INCANDESCENCE	REASSURING	FREE SPACE	AVARICE	WEARY
PETULANT	ESSENCE	THRESHED	STRENUOUS	APPREHENSIVELY
REMOTE	DISSEMBLING	RUPTURE	PERPLEXED	MONOLITHIC

The Pearl Vocabulary

PERCEPTIBLE	REASSURING	COMPARABLE	CLAMBERED	OBSCURED
WEARY	RESINOUS	ABANDONED	FRANTICALLY	REMOTE
AVARICE	PROPHECY	FREE SPACE	UNDULATING	EXHILARATION
LUCENT	TRANSFIGURED	DISCONTENTEDLY	PETULANT	MERGED
STRENUOUS	CEASELESS	DISSEMBLING	COAGULATING	LAMENT

The Pearl Vocabulary

POULTICE	RUPTURE	LETHARGY	ESSENCE	CONTEMPTUOUSLY
PRECIPITATED	JUDICIOUS	RESIDUE	MONOLITHIC	INCANDESCENCE
MONOTONOUSLY	APPREHENSIVELY	FREE SPACE	THRESHED	LAMENT
COAGULATING	DISSEMBLING	CEASELESS	STRENUOUS	MERGED
PETULANT	DISCONTENTEDLY	TRANSFIGURED	LUCENT	EXHILARATION

The Pearl Vocabulary

DISSEMBLING	WEARY	JUDICIOUS	MONOTONOUSLY	THRESHED
LUCENT	PERCEPTIBLE	ABANDONED	COAGULATING	INCANDESCENCE
REASSURING	ESSENCE	FREE SPACE	MERGED	RESINOUS
LAMENT	FRANTICALLY	CLAMBERED	COMPARABLE	BROODING
EXHILARATION	RESIDUE	MONOLITHIC	APPREHENSIVELY	AVARICE

The Pearl Vocabulary

TRANSFIGURED	RUPTURE	PERPLEXED	PETULANT	PROPHECY
REMOTE	PRECIPITATED	OBSCURED	POULTICE	CONTEMPTUOUSLY
STRENUOUS	UNDULATING	FREE SPACE	CEASELESS	AVARICE
APPREHENSIVELY	MONOLITHIC	RESIDUE	EXHILARATION	BROODING
COMPARABLE	CLAMBERED	FRANTICALLY	LAMENT	RESINOUS

The Pearl Vocabulary

CONTEMPTUOUSLY	REASSURING	JUDICIOUS	PRECIPITATED	INCANDESCENCE
COMPARABLE	DISSEMBLING	RESIDUE	FRANTICALLY	CLAMBERED
ABANDONED	PERPLEXED	FREE SPACE	UNDULATING	DISCONTENTEDLY
LETHARGY	EXHILARATION	STRENUOUS	MERGED	MONOLITHIC
RESINOUS	OBSCURED	RUPTURE	MONOTONOUSLY	PETULANT

The Pearl Vocabulary

COAGULATING	ESSENCE	POULTICE	APPREHENSIVELY	WEARY
REMOTE	LAMENT	PROPHECY	THRESHED	BROODING
AVARICE	PERCEPTIBLE	FREE SPACE	CEASELESS	PETULANT
MONOTONOUSLY	RUPTURE	OBSCURED	RESINOUS	MONOLITHIC
MERGED	STRENUOUS	EXHILARATION	LETHARGY	DISCONTENTEDLY

The Pearl Vocabulary

TRANSFIGURED	AVARICE	JUDICIOUS	POULTICE	RESINOUS
MERGED	UNDULATING	CEASELESS	STRENUOUS	RUPTURE
MONOTONOUSLY	PROPHECY	FREE SPACE	LAMENT	INCANDESCENCE
PERPLEXED	EXHILARATION	COAGULATING	CLAMBERED	WEARY
PERCEPTIBLE	THRESHED	PETULANT	FRANTICALLY	REMOTE

The Pearl Vocabulary

APPREHENSIVELY	RESIDUE	COMPARABLE	DISCONTENTEDLY	MONOLITHIC
ABANDONED	REASSURING	PRECIPITATED	LUCENT	DISSEMBLING
BROODING	LETHARGY	FREE SPACE	ESSENCE	REMOTE
FRANTICALLY	PETULANT	THRESHED	PERCEPTIBLE	WEARY
CLAMBERED	COAGULATING	EXHILARATION	PERPLEXED	INCANDESCENCE

The Pearl Vocabulary

APPREHENSIVELY	DISCONTENTEDLY	LUCENT	CEASELESS	THRESHED
BROODING	MERGED	DISSEMBLING	PERPLEXED	PROPHECY
CLAMBERED	ABANDONED	FREE SPACE	LAMENT	MONOTONOUSLY
JUDICIOUS	POULTICE	EXHILARATION	INCANDESCENCE	RESINOUS
OBSCURED	TRANSFIGURED	RUPTURE	FRANTICALLY	PERCEPTIBLE

The Pearl Vocabulary

RESIDUE	ESSENCE	COAGULATING	UNDULATING	REMOTE
STRENUOUS	CONTEMPTUOUSLY	PETULANT	AVARICE	REASSURING
WEARY	COMPARABLE	FREE SPACE	PRECIPITATED	PERCEPTIBLE
FRANTICALLY	RUPTURE	TRANSFIGURED	OBSCURED	RESINOUS
INCANDESCENCE	EXHILARATION	POULTICE	JUDICIOUS	MONOTONOUSLY

The Pearl Vocabulary

MONOLITHIC	CONTEMPTUOUSLY	DISSEMBLING	UNDULATING	PERCEPTIBLE
MERGED	FRANTICALLY	LAMENT	LUCENT	REMOTE
LETHARGY	INCANDESCENCE	FREE SPACE	AVARICE	REASSURING
WEARY	COAGULATING	COMPARABLE	OBSCURED	PRECIPITATED
JUDICIOUS	BROODING	DISCONTENTEDLY	ESSENCE	PERPLEXED

The Pearl Vocabulary

CLAMBERED	RUPTURE	PROPHECY	THRESHED	ABANDONED
STRENUOUS	TRANSFIGURED	RESIDUE	RESINOUS	APPREHENSIVELY
EXHILARATION	POULTICE	FREE SPACE	MONOTONOUSLY	PERPLEXED
ESSENCE	DISCONTENTEDLY	BROODING	JUDICIOUS	PRECIPITATED
OBSCURED	COMPARABLE	COAGULATING	WEARY	REASSURING

The Pearl Vocabulary

TRANSFIGURED	STRENUOUS	RUPTURE	ESSENCE	COMPARABLE
AVARICE	MONOLITHIC	PERPLEXED	JUDICIOUS	APPREHENSIVELY
PRECIPITATED	LUCENT	FREE SPACE	CEASELESS	PETULANT
CONTEMPTUOUSLY	UNDULATING	REMOTE	RESINOUS	POULTICE
REASSURING	PERCEPTIBLE	EXHILARATION	FRANTICALLY	DISSEMBLING

The Pearl Vocabulary

OBSCURED	COAGULATING	MONOTONOUSLY	RESIDUE	WEARY
INCANDESCENCE	ABANDONED	THRESHED	BROODING	PROPHECY
LETHARGY	CLAMBERED	FREE SPACE	MERGED	DISSEMBLING
FRANTICALLY	EXHILARATION	PERCEPTIBLE	REASSURING	POULTICE
RESINOUS	REMOTE	UNDULATING	CONTEMPTUOUSLY	PETULANT

The Pearl Vocabulary

APPREHENSIVELY	MONOLITHIC	CEASELESS	PETULANT	PRECIPITATED
THRESHED	RUPTURE	REASSURING	LAMENT	STRENUOUS
COAGULATING	MERGED	FREE SPACE	TRANSFIGURED	UNDULATING
LUCENT	DISSEMBLING	MONOTONOUSLY	CLAMBERED	RESIDUE
FRANTICALLY	DISCONTENTEDLY	BROODING	EXHILARATION	CONTEMPTUOUSLY

The Pearl Vocabulary

INCANDESCENCE	ABANDONED	ESSENCE	PERCEPTIBLE	REMOTE
JUDICIOUS	WEARY	OBSCURED	PERPLEXED	LETHARGY
PROPHECY	AVARICE	FREE SPACE	RESINOUS	CONTEMPTUOUSLY
EXHILARATION	BROODING	DISCONTENTEDLY	FRANTICALLY	RESIDUE
CLAMBERED	MONOTONOUSLY	DISSEMBLING	LUCENT	UNDULATING

The Pearl Vocabulary

REASSURING	AVARICE	COMPARABLE	BROODING	RESIDUE
INCANDESCENCE	TRANSFIGURED	LAMENT	MONOLITHIC	JUDICIOUS
POULTICE	LUCENT	FREE SPACE	ABANDONED	UNDULATING
RESINOUS	OBSCURED	DISCONTENTEDLY	PETULANT	MONOTONOUSLY
EXHILARATION	PROPHECY	CONTEMPTUOUSLY	LETHARGY	FRANTICALLY

The Pearl Vocabulary

MERGED	PRECIPITATED	PERCEPTIBLE	DISSEMBLING	RUPTURE
REMOTE	WEARY	ESSENCE	PERPLEXED	THRESHED
CLAMBERED	CEASELESS	FREE SPACE	STRENUOUS	FRANTICALLY
LETHARGY	CONTEMPTUOUSLY	PROPHECY	EXHILARATION	MONOTONOUSLY
PETULANT	DISCONTENTEDLY	OBSCURED	RESINOUS	UNDULATING

The Pearl Vocabulary

RESINOUS	AVARICE	PRECIPITATED	LAMENT	MERGED
CLAMBERED	RUPTURE	LUCENT	APPREHENSIVELY	CONTEMPTUOUSLY
BROODING	DISSEMBLING	FREE SPACE	RESIDUE	STRENUOUS
TRANSFIGURED	COMPARABLE	THRESHED	EXHILARATION	PERCEPTIBLE
OBSCURED	ABANDONED	COAGULATING	JUDICIOUS	POULTICE

The Pearl Vocabulary

PERPLEXED	CEASELESS	LETHARGY	PETULANT	INCANDESCENCE
WEARY	PROPHECY	UNDULATING	ESSENCE	MONOLITHIC
REASSURING	REMOTE	FREE SPACE	MONOTONOUSLY	POULTICE
JUDICIOUS	COAGULATING	ABANDONED	OBSCURED	PERCEPTIBLE
EXHILARATION	THRESHED	COMPARABLE	TRANSFIGURED	STRENUOUS

The Pearl Vocabulary

PETULANT	LAMENT	REASSURING	DISCONTENTEDLY	MONOLITHIC
TRANSFIGURED	UNDULATING	LUCENT	MONOTONOUSLY	OBSCURED
COMPARABLE	REMOTE	FREE SPACE	PRECIPITATED	CONTEMPTUOUSLY
ABANDONED	MERGED	CLAMBERED	PERCEPTIBLE	CEASELESS
APPREHENSIVELY	POULTICE	PERPLEXED	THRESHED	RUPTURE

The Pearl Vocabulary

PROPHECY	WEARY	EXHILARATION	FRANTICALLY	BROODING
AVARICE	STRENUOUS	RESINOUS	COAGULATING	JUDICIOUS
INCANDESCENCE	RESIDUE	FREE SPACE	ESSENCE	RUPTURE
THRESHED	PERPLEXED	POULTICE	APPREHENSIVELY	CEASELESS
PERCEPTIBLE	CLAMBERED	MERGED	ABANDONED	CONTEMPTUOUSLY

The Pearl Vocabulary

PROPHECY	COAGULATING	LETHARGY	REASSURING	JUDICIOUS
CONTEMPTUOUSLY	FRANTICALLY	UNDULATING	CLAMBERED	RESINOUS
RESIDUE	DISCONTENTEDLY	FREE SPACE	ESSENCE	ABANDONED
COMPARABLE	INCANDESCENCE	LAMENT	MONOLITHIC	THRESHED
STRENUOUS	PETULANT	CEASELESS	LUCENT	MONOTONOUSLY

The Pearl Vocabulary

WEARY	PRECIPITATED	OBSCURED	DISSEMBLING	BROODING
POULTICE	TRANSFIGURED	EXHILARATION	PERPLEXED	REMOTE
MERGED	AVARICE	FREE SPACE	RUPTURE	MONOTONOUSLY
LUCENT	CEASELESS	PETULANT	STRENUOUS	THRESHED
MONOLITHIC	LAMENT	INCANDESCENCE	COMPARABLE	ABANDONED

The Pearl Vocabulary

CEASELESS	TRANSFIGURED	PRECIPITATED	WEARY	RESIDUE
PERCEPTIBLE	APPREHENSIVELY	PROPHECY	POULTICE	LAMENT
BROODING	DISSEMBLING	FREE SPACE	PETULANT	COAGULATING
REMOTE	CONTEMPTUOUSLY	COMPARABLE	DISCONTENTEDLY	RESINOUS
MONOTONOUSLY	UNDULATING	ABANDONED	REASSURING	AVARICE

The Pearl Vocabulary

LETHARGY	PERPLEXED	JUDICIOUS	INCANDESCENCE	THRESHED
STRENUOUS	ESSENCE	FRANTICALLY	RUPTURE	CLAMBERED
OBSCURED	MONOLITHIC	FREE SPACE	EXHILARATION	AVARICE
REASSURING	ABANDONED	UNDULATING	MONOTONOUSLY	RESINOUS
DISCONTENTEDLY	COMPARABLE	CONTEMPTUOUSLY	REMOTE	COAGULATING

The Pearl Vocabulary

POULTICE	MERGED	PRECIPITATED	REMOTE	APPREHENSIVELY
CEASELESS	RUPTURE	PERPLEXED	OBSCURED	STRENUOUS
COMPARABLE	DISCONTENTEDLY	FREE SPACE	ABANDONED	RESINOUS
MONOLITHIC	BROODING	PROPHECY	CLAMBERED	ESSENCE
UNDULATING	COAGULATING	JUDICIOUS	PERCEPTIBLE	LAMENT

The Pearl Vocabulary

LUCENT	DISSEMBLING	LETHARGY	REASSURING	RESIDUE
PETULANT	MONOTONOUSLY	FRANTICALLY	CONTEMPTUOUSLY	EXHILARATION
TRANSFIGURED	THRESHED	FREE SPACE	WEARY	LAMENT
PERCEPTIBLE	JUDICIOUS	COAGULATING	UNDULATING	ESSENCE
CLAMBERED	PROPHECY	BROODING	MONOLITHIC	RESINOUS

www.ingramcontent.com/pod-product-compliance
Lightning Source LLC
LaVergne TN
LVHW081538060526
838200LV00048B/2134